MAKING MASKS

VIVIEN FRANK & DEBORAH JAFFÉ

731.75

Luton Sixth Form College
Bradgers Hill Road
Luton LU2 7EW
Telephone 01582 432480 email: library@lutonsfc.ac.uk
Return on or before the last date stamped below

WITHDRAWN

MAKING MASKS

VIVIEN FRANK & DEBORAH JAFFÉ

GE

A QUANTUM BOOK

Published by Greenwich Editions
Unit 7
202-208 New North Road
London N1 7BJ

ISBN 0-86288-091-2

This book was produced by
Quantum Books Ltd
6 Blundell Street
London N7 9BH

Creative Director: Richard Dewing
Designer: James Lawrence
Project Editors: Judith Simons/William Hemsley
Photographer: Ian Howes

Typeset in Great Britain by
Central Southern Typesetters, Eastbourne
Manufactured in Singapore by Eray Scan Pte. Ltd

Printed in Singapore by Star Standard Industries Pte. Ltd.

CONTENTS

INTRODUCTION

To don a mask is to change character. We all wear invisible masks at different times in our lives for specific situations – the brave face to cope with a difficult situation and the happy face for celebrations. Donning a mask allows the wearer to hide and to say and do things he or she might not normally do. A mask can also be protection because abuse or attack is directed at the personality of the mask not the wearer. Like a ventriloquist dummy, the wearer gives a mask life.

Achieving anonymity by wearing a mask is simple, for even the smallest concealment – covering an eye or the mouth – changes a person's appearance. Bandits, pirates and robbers have used eye patches, eye masks, and mouth masks as well as balaclavas to alter their appearance and avoid recognition.

For thousands of years different cultures throughout the world have made masks for celebrations, to ward off evil spirits, to commemorate seasonal events, for religious and pagan rituals, for dance and for self-defence. The forces of evil, power and love have all been symbolized as masks. Often

made from found, local materials, masks have been carefully crafted and sculpted to become beautiful and fantastic objects.

Most children find wearing masks great fun, loving to surprise and scare, while believing themselves to be hidden. Children can also make masks with enthusiasm, beginning with a simple eye mask or paper bag mask and progressing to more complex papier mâché masks when older. Their designs can be innovative and highly imaginative as they create a favourite animal, TV personality, monster or dragon.

Members of theatre groups as well as party planners intent on masked or

African antelope skin masks were produced by gifted craftsmen following ancient traditions.

Each mask of the Commedia dell'Arte *represents one of the standard group of characters.*

Wooden masks from Africa display striking and often intricate carving (above).

fancy dress balls, will find this book packed full of ideas. While its intention is to give readers an introduction to mask making, with projects carefully laid out in stages, it is possible for enthusiasts to develop their own masks based on the skills they have learned.

As much as they are fascinating, masks are historically and culturally interesting; a brief introduction to the history of masks follows, outlining their significance over the centuries. The main section of the book gives clear instructions on how to make many different types of masks, along with hints on how to wear and adapt them. A list of important mask collections in museums is provided at the end of the book along with a list of suppliers of mask-making materials. A useful bibliography is included for those who would like to delve deeper into this compelling folk-art form.

Masks are great fun to make and wear. We hope you have as much fun creating your own masks from this book as we have had creating the projects and ideas.

South East Asian masks using eye holes (top) and slits below the eyes (bottom).

HISTORY

The cave paintings at Lascaux in France, done by Stone Age man, showing him wearing masks of the animals he hunted, are among the earliest records we have of masks. By wearing the mask a hunter could take on the spirit of the animal and enact the scene he hoped to bring about. Some hunting tribes in parts of Africa and Alaska still perform such rituals.

In ancient Greece and Rome masks were important for physical protection as well as in the theatre. Between 700 and 675 BC the Greeks had well-armed and trained armies, equipped with a range of helmets with protective masks. The best of these was a bronze Corinthian type – a metal helmet with side pieces to cover the cheeks and sides of the face with a long nose piece down the middle. The Roman army, intent on expansion, was also well-equipped, with helmets which had masks for protection and masks for parade. Around AD 200 these were worn by the cavalry for special displays and some of the masks had female features, thought to have been worn by soldiers disguised as Amazons. Roman gladiators, protected by similar helmets and masks, performed for over 650 years throughout the Roman Empire. By 100 BC they were performing in public to huge audiences, commanding high prizes and much fame.

In the first and second centuries AD, ancient Egyptians made wonderful portrait masks out of plaster, which covered the faces of their dead. The plaster was hollowed out, placed on the face and fastened with cords at the base of the neck. Eyes were painted in on the mask and around AD 200 false glass eyes were fitted. As Christianity spread the use of burial masks ceased.

Protective masks have come a long way since the days of Anglo Saxon suits of armour. In the 1600s Italian

hunters had intricate and quite beautiful metal face masks. This century, gas masks and the visors attached to the helmets of baseball players, cricketers and policemen are all for self protection. In many inner cities around the world, cyclists are wearing masks to protect themselves from inhaling too many fumes.

Masks are often employed to ward off evil spirits and Satan. The use of dragons and the devil in their

Italian leather masks are shaped by beating the leather onto a mould.

An Italian rider's mask from about the sixteenth century. It protected the face from branches in wooded country.

craftwork and imagery is very important. In China and South East Asia the dragon mask is integral to the New Year celebrations and in dances to ward off evil spirits. In Bali, the Hindu dance of the Ramayana is cast with actors all wearing different masks to portray the powers of good and evil and their conquests.

South East Asian dragon masks (below and right) are important in many festivals and are beautiful objects in themselves.

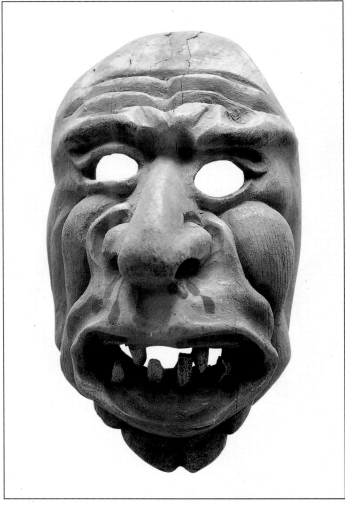

A Roman mask made of pewter, which may have been used by a priest or priestess during ceremonies.

In Austria and Switzerland tree trunks, old hats and fabric are fashioned as grotesque masks to ward off the winter spirits and welcome the spring and good weather for the crops.

The influence of Catholicism in many countries has been amalgamated with the indigenous culture to create very colourful and witty masks for carnival. The original word "carnevale" means farewell (*vale*) to meat (*carne*) in Latin. The eating of meat was forbidden during Lent and the week preceding it was a time for lots of fun and indulgence. Wherever there is carnival there are masks.

The Venetian carnival inspired *Commdia dell 'Arte*, a theatrical style originating in the sixteenth century. The cast wears half masks enabling the audience to see the expressions of their mouths. The masks are made from all kinds of materials including leather, straw, and fabric. The characters always include a Pierrot, Harlequin,

Punch, the Four Seasons, Sun and Moon.

The week before Lent is also carnival time in New Orleans where Mardi Gras or Fat Tuesday is celebrated on a grand scale. The streets are filled with floats and all kinds of masked characters appear reflecting the different ethnic groups in the city – French Mardi Gras, Black Mardi Gras and Cajun Mardi Gras. It is thought that Mardi Gras was celebrated in Paris in the Middle Ages and transported to the New World at a very early stage. On 3 March 1699, the French explorer, Iberville set up a camp on the Mississippi, south of New Orleans and called it Point du Mardi Gras. New Orleans itself was founded in 1718 and, under French rule, masked balls were held in the period before Lent. The Spanish later put an end to the tradition but when New Orleans became an American city, the Creole population demanded its reintroduction and in

A highly grotesque Austrian mask, carved from wood and painted, which was used at Alpine festivals.

Masks used at the Venetian carnival are part of a tradition reaching back to the sixteenth century.

1827 masks were allowed in the streets once again. Full street carnival developed from this time.

Pre-Lenten carnival is very important in Trinidad and Tobago and in Brazil, particularly Rio, when masks form an integral part of huge and very ornate costumes. In Britain, the Caribbean community in the Notting Hill area of west London, holds a carnival each year at the end of August lasting three days. This is a huge event attracting hundreds of thousands of people with hundreds of characters parading around in various guises.

Many African masks are finely carved from wood and take the form of stylized faces.

In Africa masks are made from antelope skin, straw and wood. They are beautiful examples of craftwork taking a long time to make. The Yoruba in Nigeria believe a mask can be as simple as a piece of cloth to cover the face or as complicated as a full face, carefully carved, wooden mask. In Zaire, hats with fabric hanging from the brim in front of the face are masks.

In the nineteenth century there was a large mask-making tradition among the Inuit of North America. These ranged from partial and whole face masks to masks covering the entire body. They had a fantastic range of expressions and many were asymmetrical, where the eyes might not be level, while others were half animal and half man. Some looked like birds and mythical creatures.

The basic mask was made of driftwood, sculpted and decorated with an array of found materials – twigs and sticks, feathers, string and bone all used to great effect. Some masks were left bare and the grain of the wood used to accentuate facial features. Feathers were used to give movement and paint was used sparingly. Each mask had terrific presence and beauty, reflecting great imagination and skill on the part of its creator.

The Inuit used masks for religious and secular activities. The masks were made to symbolize good and bad mythological beings in the creation of the world, the destroyers of that world, gods, spirits, the sun and moon. Essential to the masks's function was the shaman who wore the mask and in a trance state made it come to life. Sometimes the shaman made his, or in some cases her, own masks, although usually they were made by specialist mask makers. This tradition of mask making and carving is still alive today.

Tribes throughout Africa, as well as the North American Indians, the Australian Aborigines and the New Zealand Maoris have traditionally decorated their faces and bodies with paint and tattoos. These forms of decoration could be called masks – they are used for a number of reasons, including attraction, membership to a particular group or tribe, fertility rites, and initiation ceremonies.

In the Lancashire and Yorkshire area of England, mummers appear each New Year's Eve. Groups of children and adults dress up, the males as females and the females as males, and cover their faces with black paint. Each has a sweeping brush and does not speak but makes a humming sound. They go from house to house sweeping out the old year, making their humming sound. The best mummers enter the house from the front and leave by the back door leaving the house free of spirits. Their disguise is so perfect the householders have no idea who they really are.

The application of make-up to the face transforms many women, making them feel more attractive and confident. But it could be argued that make-up is just another form of masking, since it hides the person underneath. Men grow a variety of moustaches and beards which all change the face, sometimes almost

In a modern production of the ancient Greek play The Oresteia *the actors are all wearing masks.*

beyond recognition, and can be used as a very effective form of disguise.

The famous wear dark glasses to make themselves anonymous. Indeed spectacles can alter a person's face making it look sophisticated and powerful, stupid or intelligent. Spectacles are not worn just for opthalmic reasons – Groucho Marx, Dame Edna Everidge and Elton John would not be the same characters without their idiosyncratic glasses.

Masks and disguise must include the Hallowe'en witch. Although much has been written about the wrongs done against women thought to be witches, she still remains a mysterious character. Beneath the black conical hat her wizened face, pointed nose, blackened and decayed teeth and straggling hair are fantastic material for the mask maker.

The surgeon's mask protects patients undergoing surgery, at the same time giving him special status and mystery. The bride and widow wear veils to hide their faces. The bride's veil makes her more seductive and denotes virginity while the widow's veil gives privacy in her sorrow.

The actor's mask has a very old history. Ancient Greeks were the first to use masks for performance. The narrator would use different masks to represent the various characters and each mask would indicate who was speaking. The word "hypocrite" derives from the Greek word "hyporites" meaning actor; as he often wore a mask he was therefore two-faced.

Noh theatre in Japan dates back to the twelfth century. Each Noh mask, in its simplicity, shows a different spirit. The plays deal with the spiritual, the supernatural, demons and ghosts and are still performed today.

People as diverse as Shakespeare and Walt Disney have made use of the power of the mask, from Bottom in *A Midsummer Night's Dream* wearing an ass's head to Mickey Mouse made up of a complicated full head mask – and everything in between. Modern actors on both film and stage use a vast array of masks using diverse materials from traditioinal make-up and human-hair wigs to the latest plastics technology. Mask making is a tradition and its history continues to evolve.

A plain modern manufactured mask can act as a canvas onto which an infinite variety of characters and expressions can be painted.

TECHNIQUES

The masks in this book are to a great extent suitable for most people to wear. In a few cases the masks have been specially designed to suit children or adults and this fact has been noted in the instructions, but in general the masks can be adapted to accommodate various sizes.

If you have never made a mask before it would be wise to start with one of the simpler styles at the beginning of the project section. However it is quite unnecessary to work through all the methods in the technique section before starting on a mask. This section is intended to operate as a reference area for the various ways of creating masks.

The template section, starting on page 112, has most of the templates and patterns for the masks in the book. Some of these are shown full-size and some will need to be enlarged; this is explained and information is also given on ways of altering sizes.

There are some general rules about faces which apply to everyone. Look at the face of any adult and you will see that the eyes are situated approximately halfway between the top of the head and the chin. In young children the eyes are a little lower. You will notice that the bottom of the nose lies halfway between the eyes and the chin, with the mouth coming halfway between nose and chin. The ears fit between the levels of the eyes and the bottom of the nose.

Positioning eye holes in the mask is one of the most important and difficult things to do. They should not be made too large because too much of the wearer's own eyes would show and this might detract from the effect of the mask. On the other hand if they are too small the wearer will be unable to see properly. In some masks, notably in Mexico and South America, the eye holes of the masks are slits cut into the mask at a place to suit the wearer but they bear no relation to the design of the mask, which is elaborately decorated. One way of minimizing the effect caused by large eye holes is to make a feature of them by sticking net across the space. This will enable the wearer to see quite clearly but will completely shield the eyes and expression from the audience.

Gloriously coloured paints characterize many South East Asian masks.

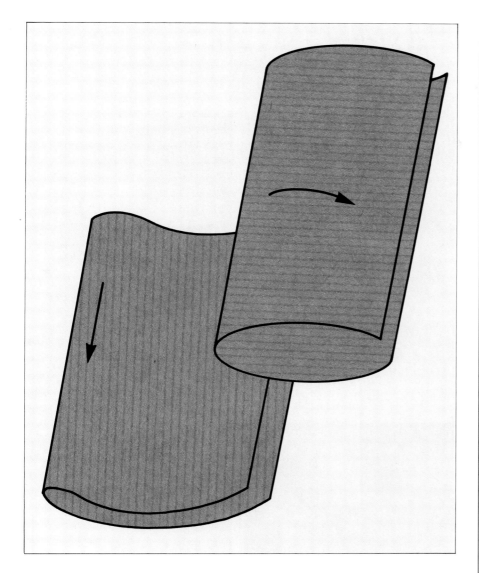

weighs between 80 and 120gsm. For the purposes of this book the paper will be divided into two categories – light-weight and medium-weight. Light-weight papers include tissue, tracing and decorative Japanese papers and cover any paper up to about 150gsm. Medium-weight papers are those papers between 150 and 230gsm. Above this weight the material will be referred to in this book as card, although some art suppliers may call it heavy-weight paper.

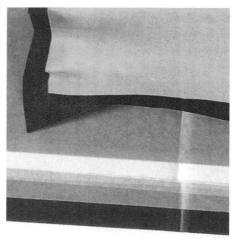

PAPER PROPERTIES

Many of the masks in this book have been made from paper and card and several of them have been decorated with paper. In order to take advantage of all the possibilities, there are two facts about paper and card which it will be useful to know. Paper and card have a grain and this direction should be ascertained in order to use the material to advantage. Paper and card are usually measured by weight and this is expressed by grammes per square metre – g/m^2 or gsm.

To find out which direction the grain runs in any piece of paper, lay the sheet on a flat surface. Bend the paper over on itself from the side and press gently with the hand. Repeat this action bending the paper from top to bottom. It will bend more easily in the direction of the grain – see diagram. Card should be held in the middle of the sides and flexed. Then turn the sheet of card through 90 degrees and repeat. As with paper, the card will flex more easily in the direction of the grain. In the project section of the book you will sometimes find that one of the dimensions of the paper measurements is underlined. This has been done in cases where it is important that the grain runs correctly and the underlined number indicates the grain direction.

It is important to know a little about the weights of paper and card so you can select the right materials for your chosen project. The easiest way to understand about paper weight is to refer to a familiar paper. For example, photocopy or writing paper usually

DECORATIVE TECHNIQUES

Cutting

Paper and card can be cut with a craft knife but the surface on which you are cutting must be protected either with a cutting mat or, if that is not available, scrap card or old newspapers.

Paper can also be cut with scissors but remember to keep separate scissors for paper and fabric. If you are cutting a curve try to move the paper around as the scissors are closing but held in the same position. This will ensure a smooth curve. For a decorative effect pinking shears can be used.

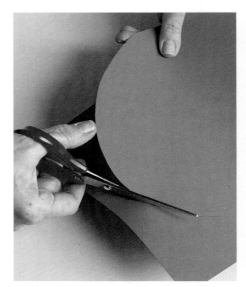 

Tearing

This technique is suitable for any weight of paper. It is useful to know the grain direction when tearing paper because a smoother edge will result if the paper is torn in the same direction as the grain. It is also possible to control the tear. When tearing the paper against the grain a more jagged edge will appear.

DECORATIVE TECHNIQUES

Punching

This is an easy and effective way of decorating paper or card. It can be done with big or small holes. There are several types of hole punch available including the single hole punch bought at a stationery shop, the revolving head hole punch normally associated with leather work and the type used in conjunction with rivets (if using this type make sure the work surface is protected). Draw faint pencil lines and try to punch the holes evenly.

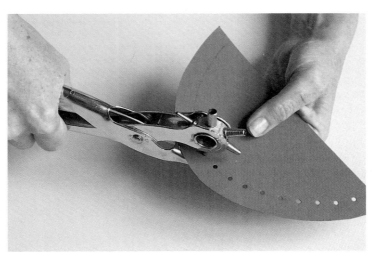

Scoring

This technique is very useful and will help give a professional finish to many projects, as a scored line will bend more easily. The purpose of scoring is to open up one side of the paper by drawing a line with a blunt point. This can be the scissor points or the back of a cutting knife, but care should be taken not to cut through the paper. Sometimes, with thick card such as that used for the horse's head mask (see page 105), it is necessary to cut through half of the thickness of the card and bend away from the cut. It would be wise to practise this on a scrap piece of the card being used for the project.

DECORATIVE TECHNIQUES

Pleating

This is another way of using paper for decorative purposes. The folds will crease more crisply if they are made with the grain, where possible. If accuracy is required, the position of the folds can be measured prior to folding, and scoring the lines will make the process of creasing easier.

 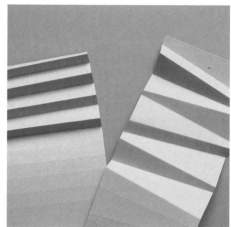

Rolling

Paper can be rolled around various objects and held in place with some form of adhesive, depending on the final use of the roll. Rolls can vary from pencil size to large cylinders. As with the previous method the roll will be best achieved if created with the grain. This applies especially in the case of whole head masks, such as the lion's head (see page 102).

Curling

To make paper curls, cut the paper against the grain and then pull the strips, one by one, across the back of a knife, scissor blade or ruler – this causes the paper to stretch on one side and thus curl. Practise with different paper weights to discover what works best for your purpose.

Scrunching

This is a fun method but is best suited to very light-weight papers. Cut or tear the paper into squares or triangles and screw up the pieces. This can be done tightly or loosely and the resulting shape can be glued in position where required – sometimes a little glue may be added to the shape.

FASTENINGS AND FIXINGS

There are numerous ways of attaching pieces of paper, card and fabric together. Some of these ways are listed here but you will probably think of other methods. Some of the methods are suitable only as a temporary measure but they are still important, particularly when an extra pair of hands is unavailable!

Adhesive tapes

There are three main types of adhesive tape – masking tape, which has low tack and is extremely useful for temporary fixing and usually does not mark the material which is being held; normal adhesive tape which is usually sold under a brand name; and double-sided adhesive tape which is excellent for creating invisible bonding.

Glues

There are many types of glue available and each person has his or her own favourite brand. In this book we have used mainly PVA adhesive, sometimes called white glue or school glue. This glue is clean to use, it dries transparent and allows the user time to position the parts being attached. Sometimes a quick-drying glue is required and for this purpose one of the proprietary brands of clear glue is suggested.

Staples

These are very useful for joining parts together quickly but be sure to cover the open ends with tape if they are anywhere near the face.

Paper clips

Extremely handy for holding various parts together temporarily.

Paper fasteners

These can also be used in a temporary or permanent way but remember that quite a large hole is required in which to insert the fastener prior to opening out the points. The advantage of this type of fixing is that it allows movement of the parts attached. Again

it would be wise to tape over the open ends of the fasteners if they are to be used for any length of time.

Needle and thread

Sometimes a needle and thread may be the easiest way of joining two parts. This may be particularly appropriate when attaching two dissimilar materials, such as fabric to card. The thread used must be strong enough to support whatever is being attached, so choose a thread which will not break easily, such as button thread.

Slots and tabs

These are methods of creating fixings without using any other material. A slot is cut into one piece of material and a tab is added to the other piece of material. This tab is then pushed through the slot. Sometimes glue or adhesive tape can also be used to create a more permanent fixing. If the card is thick it may actually be necessary to cut out a sliver of card from the slot to accommodate the tab.

SAFETY

At all times be aware of safety factors. Make sure that children are always under supervision.

When using craft knives and hole punches always work on a surface which is protected with a cutting mat or thick scrap card.

Never pierce the eye holes when the mask is in front of the face or over the head. Always mark the eye positions with a pencil and then remove the mask from the head before cutting the holes.

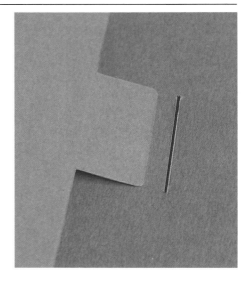

METHODS OF FIXING MASKS

There are several ways of fixing masks so that they can be worn comfortably. Sometimes the type of mask dictates the method of fixing as with the Rider mask (see page 75) but, as a general rule, the best way to choose a method is to experiment with all the ways of fixing and select which one suits you the best.

Elastic, string or ribbon attached to the mask at about the level of the eyes is the easiest and most common way of fixing the mask.

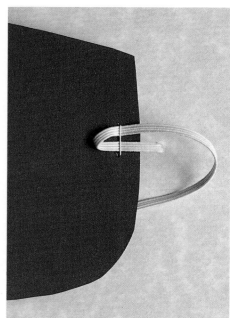

Method 1 – Elastic

If fixing the elastic by piercing a hole and tying, always strengthen the area of the mask where the hole has been made so that the weakness caused by the hole is reduced. This can be done by sticking masking tape over the hole area on the inside of the mask so that the decoration of the mask is unaffected. Alternatively, staple the elastic in position and cover the staples with layers of adhesive tape for the wearer's protection.

The most suitable and comfortable type of elastic to use is hat/millinery/round cord elastic but thin, flat elastic can be used if this type is not available.

Two elastic bands looped through the holes in the mask and stretched around the ears can be used as an impromptu fixing although this may not be comfortable to wear for a long period of time.

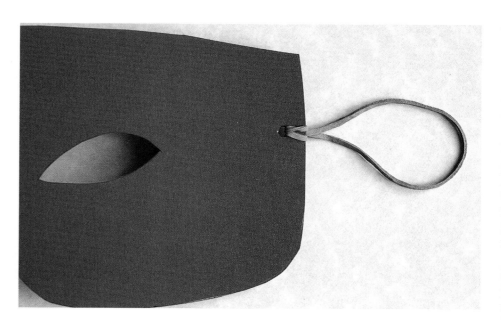

TIP
If there are spots where a mask rubs the face or otherwise feels uncomfortable, it is quite easy to stick a piece of soft material, such as stockinette, to the inside of the mask using glue or tape.

METHODS OF FIXING MASKS

Method 2 – String

If you decide to use string make sure that the knot securing the string to the inside of the mask is larger than the hole, or use staples. In either case stick a piece of adhesive tape over the ends to keep them in place. The string can be painted to match or contrast either with the hair of the wearer or with the design of the mask.

Method 3 – Ribbon

Thin black cotton ribbon was traditionally used in Victorian masks but more exotic ribbons can be used as part of the decorative effect of a mask, for example in the Masked ball mask (see page 48). The ribbon can be held in place with staples but make sure the ends are covered with tape so that they do not scratch the face.

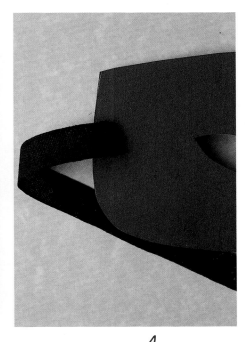

Method 4 – Sticks

This is a useful way of fixing a mask when it does not need to be kept permanently in front of the face. There are two ways of using sticks.

Style A If the mask is a flat whole face mask, such as the Dragon mask (see page 82), a flat piece of wood can be attached centrally to the chin area of the mask. The stick should be stuck in place with glue and the glued end covered with adhesive tape. This method is good for young children.

Style B If the mask is an eye/domino mask, such as the Masked ball mask (see page 48), a small round stick is normally used. This can be fixed with glue and/or tape at the side of the mask or slotted through two holes (see diagram). The stick can be painted or decorated to suit the mask.

In both instances the length of the stick will depend upon the person carrying the mask, but it is wisest to make the stick too long and cut it down to size as required.

Method 5

When making an oversize mask, such as the Dragon mask on page 82, a different method is required. A quick and easy way is created by using strips made from light-weight card.

Take a strip of card about 1in/2cm wide and fix this around the head of the person who will be wearing the mask and secure this ring with adhesive tape.

Next fix another strip at right angles to the ring and place the ring back on the head. The second strip should be at the centre back.

Bring the loose end over the crown of the head and fix it at the front so that it sits comfortably. This headgear, when firmly taped, can be fixed centrally to an oversize mask and will be most comfortable to wear.

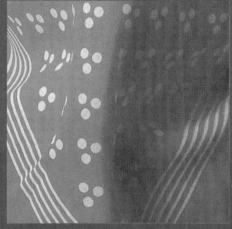

PARTIAL MASKS
USING ACCESSORIES

SCARF

A scarf is an important part of disguise and mask making. It can be wound round the head and face in numerous ways. For the Yoruba in Nigeria a mask can be as simple as a piece of cloth covering the whole head and face. A pirate might wear a scarf over his mouth and nose.

The type of fabric, its colour and pattern all change a scarf disguise. A piece of plain black cloth implies something sinister while a piece of thin voile in a delicate colour and print means something magical and fairylike.

● 1yd/1m square of black net covering the head and face.

● One black scarf covering the mouth and nose and another covering the head, with only the eyes visible.

● Red spotted handkerchief over the mouth, fastened at the back, giving the look of a bandit.

GLITZY GLASSES

Spectacles and sunglasses can form the basis of an eye mask. Using suitable glue and paints they can be quickly transformed and when combined with a moustache, coloured teeth and a plastic nose they can make moveable masks.

MATERIALS

- old spectacles or sunglasses

- glue suitable for plastics

- sequins

- long pin or matchstick

Preparation

1. Make sure the lenses are clean. Carefully put a thin layer of glue around the top of the frames and stick sequins on it, using a pin or matchstick to help put them in place. Put a little more glue on top of the sequins. Stick more sequins onto this to build up a thick layer.

TIP

Try making "Funny Eye Spectacles" by painting the shape of an eye with white enamel paint onto the dark lenses and sticking false eyelashes around them.

2. Put glue around the rest of the lens, up to the frame. Stick on sequins. Stick an odd sequin on the lens. Leave the glasses to dry.

ORANGE-SKIN TEETH

This is a very old-fashioned type of disguise which looks effective, gruesome and amusing at the same time. It is particularly useful at Hallowe'en. Peel the orange carefully. If possible do this by dividing the orange skin into six segments. Lay one of the pieces, orange side upmost, on the cutting mat and slice through the centre, leaving ½in/1cm uncut at each end. Now cut jagged teeth on either side of the slit. Place the orange skin in your mouth between lips and teeth and look to see whether you like the result. You have five other possible sets on which to practise or to make for your friends.

CARD FRAME SPECTACLES

Another spectacle disguise can be achieved by making frames from card and decorating them in whatever style appeals to you – this could be severe and heavy-looking or it could be stylish and extravagant.

Many different decorative materials can be used and the only limitation is your imagination. The exotic styles shown here are simply extensions of the basic shape. You will find all three templates on page 113 and you could experiment with the basic shape yourself to create your own styles.

Preparation

1. Trace the pattern from the templates and draw it onto the card. If you are using foil card draw onto the wrong side. Cut out the card frames.

2. If you are using the shorter piece of card it will be necessary to fix the arms with adhesive tape. This should be done before decorating so that the tape can be hidden as much as possible – decoration can be stuck over the tape.

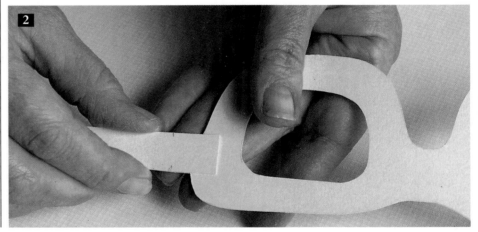

3. Now begins the fun of decorating. The basic shape has been adorned with strung sequins as they can be glued in curls and twists quite easily.

MATERIALS

- spectacles template page 113

- pencil

- tracing paper

- stiff card for the basic shapes 17in × 5in/42cm × 13cm or 7½in × 4in/18cm × 10cm

- craft knife

- glitter pens, sequins, feathers, net, tissue paper, pipe cleaners etc

- clear glue and adhesive tape

● The spiky shape looks extremely glamorous, made here with foil card of 11in × 5½in/28cm × 14cm. The mask could be lavishly decorated with fake jewels, or various other colours of foil card can be glued on.

● The butterfly glasses are cut from card of 7½in × 5in/18cm × 12cm. They have been decorated with glitter paints, strung sequins and sequins. Adding net "lenses" aids the delicate style. A toning pipe-cleaner has been pushed through the middle of the top and twisted so that it stays in place.

FACE PAINTING

Decorating and painting the face makes a mask. Throughout the world
different cultures have used this method as part of their mask making. North
American Indians painted beautiful patterns on their faces, while in parts of
Africa tattooing and face painting are still practised.

MATERIALS

- a range of face paints and crayons

- old lipsticks and rouge

- cleansing cream

- cotton wool

- cotton buds

- hair band or scarf to fasten hair away from the face

The use of face paints and make-up is very important in the theatre. The simple application of eye make-up and lipstick to accentuate an actress's features can make her look more beautiful or ugly, younger or older. A skilled make-up artist can paint lifelike wounds and scars, wrinkles and beauty spots on a face.

The clown uses face painting to change his face completely, enlarging his mouth and lips, drawing shapes round his eyes and on his cheeks to make a face which immediately tells us he is a clown. A mime artist tries to minimize the face by covering it in white face paint adding just a little detail, usually in black, around the eyes. This minimalist effect allows him to use his face to express any emotion he wants, being happy or sad depending on the way he uses his mask.

TIPS

- Use only face paints, face crayons and make-up, *never* ordinary paint. Have cotton wool and face cleanser on hand to clean the face afterwards.

- You might want to combine face painting with a partial mask. An eye mask for a ball, for example, might require painted lips and a beauty spot.

- The winter eye mask (see page 50) could be worn on a frozen face – painted white and pale blue.

- The full face, dragon's head (see page 82) might want a painted nose and lips.

- A witch (see page 64) combines many mask components – hat and nose – and requires good, dark, spooky make-up to make her come alive.

DUAL FACE

You can paint the two halves of the face in whatever colour you wish, making sure they are strong enough in contrast to be noticeable. Draw a thin line in the darker of the two colours down the middle of the face. Fill in the lighter half of the face first then the darker half. Accentuate the eyes and outline the mouth with a thin black line or apply dark lipstick to the lips.

Preparation

● Before applying make-up or face paint decide on the character you want to create and study a picture of the face and its features carefully. Either copy one of the designs given here or create your own, but practise first on the outline drawing of the face.

● After you have selected your character you can start on the real face. Tie your hair back in a hairband or scarf and make sure your face is clean. Apply the foundation or base colour first. Some characters will not need this as the bare flesh will be the base colour.

● Accentuate the eyes.

● You may want to paint in other features on the face.

● Do your mouth last.

● Look at the face and make any minor adjustments.

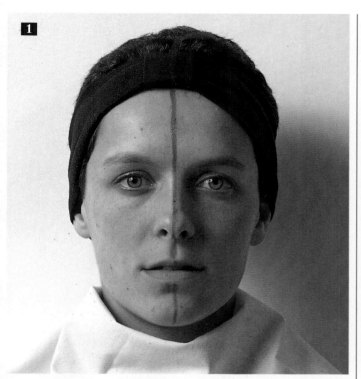

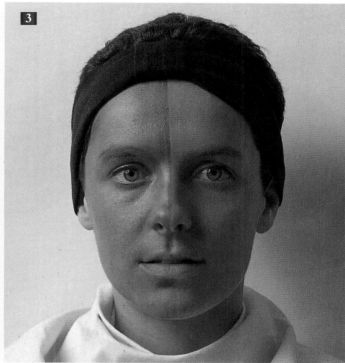

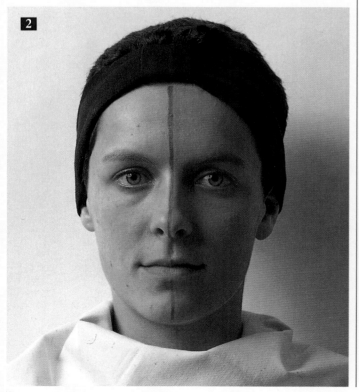

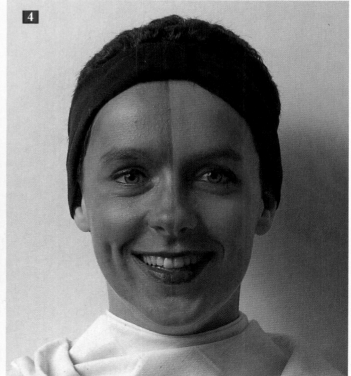

BEAUTY

Leave skin flesh colour, or apply a little foundation. Accentuate eyebrows. Apply eyeshadow and shape the eyes with thin black lines. Use false eyelashes or paint in eyelashes in black on lower lid. Put rouge and a beauty spot on the cheeks. Accentuate the lips with red glossy lipstick.

CAT

Look at the face carefully and work out where the stripes will go. Select your base colour. White is a good base colour and ginger, brown and grey are good for stripes. Draw in lines for the stripes, fill in pale areas, including the lips, and then dark areas. Paint in a small rectangle on the tip of the nose. Draw in the whiskers in black, or you could add paper whiskers.

PIERROT

Draw in the shapes with a thin black
line. Fill in the white area then the
shapes in black. Paint the lips black.

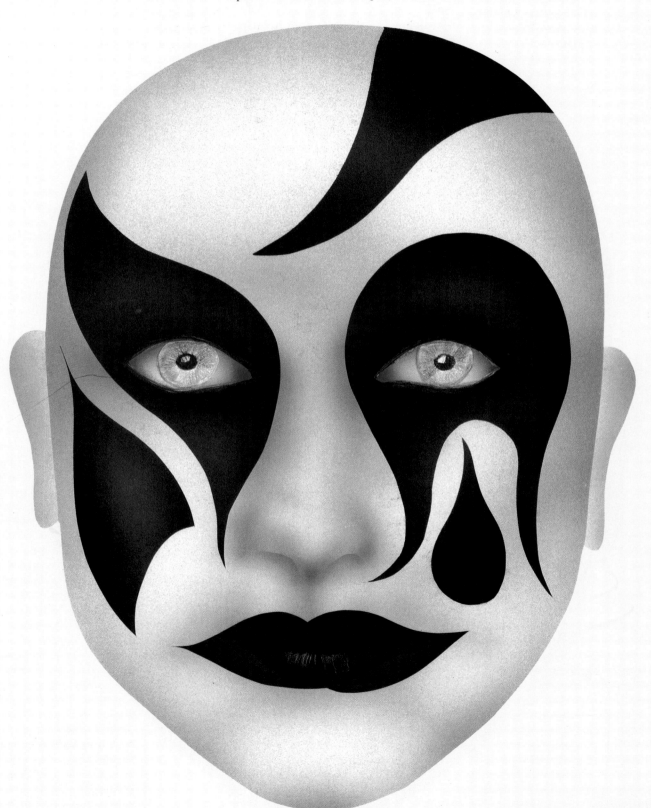

CLOWN
NUMBER 1

Leave skin flesh colour or cover in white. Draw the outlines of the shapes around the eyes and fill in. Accentuate the eyes by drawing thin black lines around them. Paint a large red circle on the end of the nose. Draw in the lips.

CLOWN NUMBER 2

A different clown's face, more angular and austere, but still filled with life and laughter. The steps for producing this face are shown opposite.

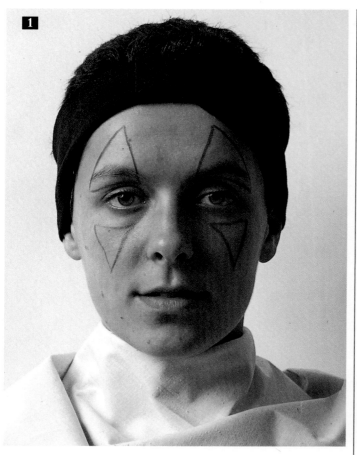

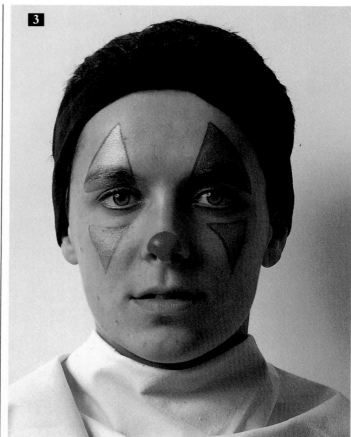

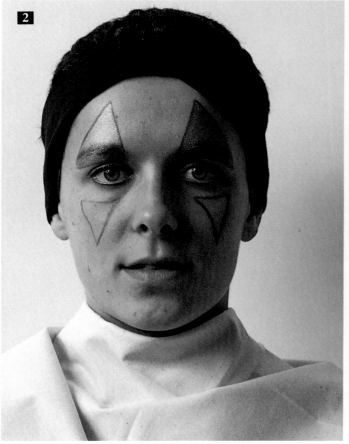

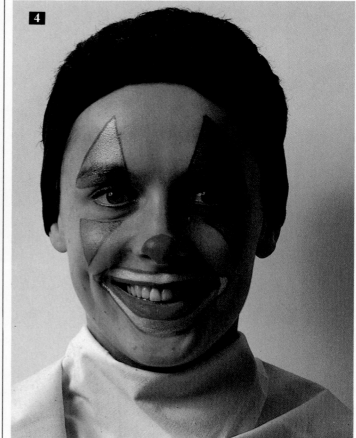

EYE PATCH

The first requisite of any pirate is an eye patch. It makes him look more powerful and mysterious. Although people have to wear eye patches as a result of injury or illness, for some reason an eye patch does seem to convey status and mystery. For example, Moshe Dayan, the famous Israeli states-man in the 1960s and 1970s always wore a black eye patch. He was instantly recognizable and seemed confident and mysterious.

Preparation

1. Using white chalk, draw round the eye patch template onto card or felt. **2.** Cut out the shape.

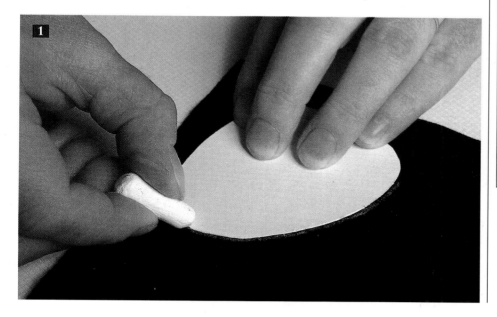

MATERIALS
■ eye patch template (see page 114)
■ lightweight black card or black felt
■ white chalk or fabric-marking pencil
■ millinery elastic or narrow black ribbon
■ needle and black cotton

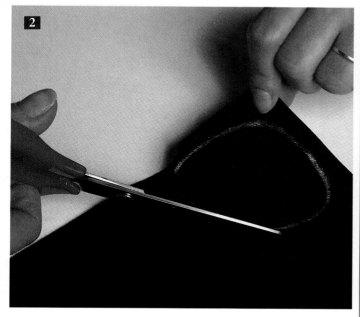

3. Make holes for the elastic thread. Pass the elastic through, knotting it at either end on the back of the patch. If you are using felt you might like to stitch two lengths of ribbon to the back of the patch, where the punched holes for the elastic would be (see techniques section page 20).

PARTIAL MASKS

BURGLAR BILL

Burglar Bill is the archetypal thief. He can wear this black eye mask on its own or combine it with a knitted face-mask (see page 96), a scarf (see page 24) or an old flat cap.

Preparation

1. Decide whether the mask is to be made out of card or felt. Trace round the template with pencil onto the card, or with white chalk on the felt.

2. Cut out the mask using scissors or a craft knife. Cut out the eye holes as well at this stage.

3. For the fastening use method 3 (see page 19). You might decide to stitch black ribbon elastic to the sides of the mask in line with the eye holes.

MATERIALS

■ eye mask template 1 page 115

■ medium-weight black card 10in × 4in/25cm × 10cm or black felt the same size

■ white chalk

■ pencil

■ scissors

■ craft knife

TIP

As this is a basic mask, you could cut it out of white or coloured card and decorate it with felt pens and paint for a different character.

MASKED BALL

A masked ball is great fun. We are never quite sure who is underneath the mask. You can cover this mask in sequins or scrunched paper or a mixture of both decorations.

MATERIALS

- eye mask template (page 115)

- metallic foil card 10in × 4in/ 25cm × 10cm

- sequins

- scrunched tissue paper

- PVA glue

- pencil

- craft knife and scissors

Preparation

1. Draw round the template onto the card and cut out the mask. Cut out the eye holes. Put a thin layer of PVA glue around one of the eye holes and cover with sequins.

2. Put a little more PVA on top of this and some more sequins. When all is dry, put a thin layer of PVA on any loose sequins. The glue is colourless when it dries.

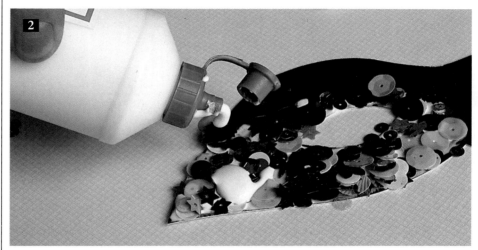

3. Either repeat step 2 above on the other eye hole, or dip the bottom of scrunched pieces of paper in glue and stick them around the eye hole.

Use method 3 for fixing or, if you want to add further excitement to the mask, attach a stick to the back of the mask using method 4b.

TIP

There are many decorative variations of this mask; you could use small coloured buttons or beads instead of sequins. Curl chenille lengths around a pencil and stick them to the top of the mask to make antennae.

THE FOUR SEASONS

The portrayal of the seasons is very important in the Venetian Commedia
dell 'Arte *as well as in the various medieval books of days. By using a
mixture of natural and artificial materials you can make a series of very rich
seasonal eye masks.*

MATERIALS

- eye mask template 3

- PVA glue

- craft knife and scissors

- pencil

Spring
- medium-weight light yellow or light green card 10in × 5in/25cm × 12cm

- small dried or artificial flowers in light colours

- artificial leaves

Summer
- medium-weight white card 10in× 5in/25cm × 12cm

- artificial or dried flowers in bright colours

- feather butterfly – optional

Autumn
- medium-weight white card 10in × 5in/25cm × 12cm

- dried leaves, rosehips

- dried flowers in brown and ochre colours

- dried barley, oats or wheat

- small artificial berries in orange, yellow and purple.

Winter
- medium-weight pale purple or pale blue metallic card 10in × 5in/25cm × 12cm

- dried moss

- dried leaves

- white paint and brush

- silver spray paint

Each of the four masks uses the same mask template. Their decoration will depend on the materials you have available. For spring you may have to rely on artificial flower buds and in summer there may be brightly coloured dried flowers available. If it is autumn you may be able to gather crisp leaves, dried flower heads and rosehips from the garden and barley and oats from a farmer. Winter requires twigs and evergreen shrubbery and some bright berries which can be artificial.

There are a number of suppliers of artificial-flower-making components and it is great fun to see what you can do with artificial stamens, petals and leaves. Many craft and gift shops sell dried flowers and a small bunch, once dismantled, will go a long way in mask making.

Preparation

1. Select the season you are going to make and draw round the template onto the appropriate card. Cut out the eye shapes. Build up the mask gradually. Attach leaves and larger flowers first by dipping them in PVA glue and sticking them onto the mask. Let them overlap the edge of the mask.

2. Put on the smaller bits like buds, small flowers and fruits last.

Spring

Spring is evoked by light, fresh, clean colours.

Summer

Deep, rich, vibrant colours represent summer.

Autumn

*Autumn is a time of
faded, mellow, warm
colours.*

Winter

*Silver gives a sense of the
cold, brittle hardness of
winter.*

3. Look at your mask carefully to see that it evokes the right season; make any adjustments. Check that you can see through the eye holes and if necessary trim away any excess foliage. Use method 1 or 4 for fixing.

4. For the winter mask, paint the leaves white before sticking them down then put moss around them. Leave some of the card bare and spray the whole thing with a thin layer of silver spray paint.

TIP

You can use this method to make a bird mask by covering the white card blank with feathers and the occasional sequin.

EYES AND EARS MASK

The two masks shown here are both made from the same basic pattern and you will probably think of other animals which can be created from the same template. Both cat and mouse can be made from a variety of coloured card or indeed the card could be painted to create a tabby effect. The important thing to remember is that you are trying to represent the essentials of the animal — a mouse has large ears with pink inside; a black cat has often got green eyes and cats generally have pointed ears.

Preparation

1. Trace the patterns from the single template on page 116. Draw the pattern onto the appropriate card and cut out carefully, trying to make the curves as smooth as you possibly can.

2. Cut out the ear linings from the coloured paper.

3. Stick the ear linings in place centrally on the ears.

MATERIALS

- animal template page 116

- pencil, scissors and craft knife

- tracing paper

- light- to medium-weight card in grey and black 11¾in × 8¼in/ 29cm × 21cm

- scraps of pink, pale grey and green paper or card

- glue

- elastic or ribbon

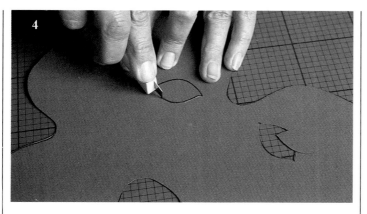

4. Cut out eye holes using the craft knife on a protected surface.

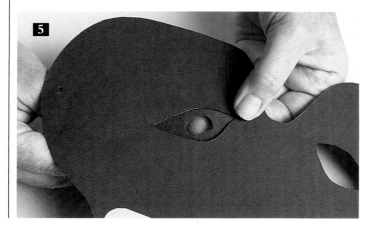

5. For the cat, cut scraps of green paper which will stick behind the eye hole and cut a much smaller hole in the centre of each piece. Make holes on the sides of the mask for the elastic and tie to fit.

HARLEQUIN MASK

This style of mask can be made to look very spectacular, offering ample opportunity for lavish use of decorative materials. In this example a variety of paper and card has been used including foil and fluorescent, patterned and coloured paper. In addition, pieces of leather and fabric have been introduced – a marvellous way of using off-cuts and leftovers from other projects. Traditionally the Harlequin is dressed in patchwork and this is why the costume is made up of differently coloured squares.

Preparation

1. Trace the pattern from the template section and enlarge using the grid system explained in that chapter. Draw the pattern onto the wrong side of the card and cut out very carefully.

If you are using foil card for the basic shape it will be necessary to cut the face area from some plain white card first then stick the foil in position on the main shape. The dotted lines on the template indicate this area. If you are using plain card you will only need to mark this area with a pencil.

2. A diamond grid with the shapes 1½in/4cm apart has been used in this example but this is quite arbitrary and other designs or measurements can be substituted. First mark your chosen design onto the right side of the card. Then cut up lots of pieces of decorative materials so that they will fit within the grid and arrange them.

3. When sticking the shapes in place, continue right to the edges. Cut away the excess areas from the wrong side when you have finished.

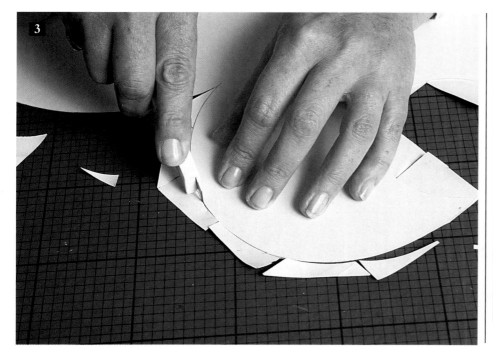

MATERIALS

- harlequin template page 118
- pencil and ruler
- scissors and craft knife
- tracing paper
- card for mask, about 20in × 20in/50cm × 50cm
- clear glue and adhesive tape
- materials for decorating
- strips of card 1in/2cm wide for head fixing

4. To give a neat appearance, braid or other materials may be stuck over the joins between the shapes.

5. When the decoration is finished, the nose piece can be fixed in place. First score along the line marked on the pattern and then curve the nose gently and stick in place on the rear side of the face piece.

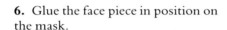

6. Glue the face piece in position on the mask.

7. Now cut out the eye holes. Finally make the head fixing following the instructions on page 19.

CROWNS AND CORONETS

Kings, queens and princesses are incomplete without crowns and coronets.
This simple mask can be lavishly decorated to become a crown or more
simply made into a coronet (as shown here) for a young princess. You could
have a royal family celebration.

MATERIALS

- crown coronet template (see page 117

- light-weight white card 9in × 6in/23cm × 15cm

- light-weight metallic card in gold, silver or bronze 13in × 7in/33cm × 20cm

- craft knife

- hole punch

- adhesive tape

- double-sided tape

- glue

- sequins, sequin strips, beads, jewels, coloured papers

- paints and paint brush

- thin ribbon for mask fastening

- soft white net or silver foil film for a veil (optional)

Preparation

1. Draw round coronet part of the template onto the wrong side of the metallic card and cut it out. Draw round face piece onto white card and cut it out. Then cut out the eyes. Try on this part of the mask and make any necessary adjustments to the nose and cheek areas. Paint in the facial details. The princess should be delicate and feminine. (See face painting page 32.)

2. Cut thin pieces of sequin strip about 3in/8cm long to make a fringe. (You could use paper strips for this, even curling some of them. See techniques section page 16.) Put double-sided tape along the top of the face part and carefully lay the sequin strip on this.

3. The coronet can be decorated in many different ways. Treat each segment in a uniform way. The princess will want simple decoration, some silver-sprayed flowers (use small silk flowers or flower-making components), plastic pearl beads and some filigree along the edges.

4. When you have finished decorating, lay the coronet over the face part, then making sure it is in position, gently press it down. The double-sided tape should hold it in place while you turn it over and tape it firmly on the back. Attach some ribbon to the back of the mask for the fastening (see techniques section page 19).

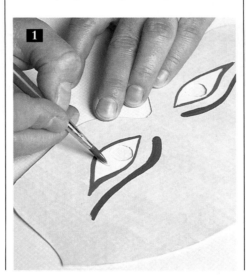

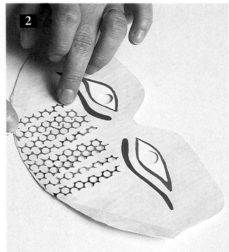

● Give a king strong bold eyebrows and eyes. You might want to put a few wrinkles around his eyes or give him a moustache using face paints. On his crown use big plastic gems, or stick on cut pieces of coloured foil card and scrunched tissue paper, sprayed gold and silver.

● If you want to make the princess more magical and fairy-like you could give her a veil. Real bridal net is very expensive but you could use cheap dress net. The quantity will depend on the size of the princess and how long you want the veil. Lay the net on top of the head and let it hang down the sides and back. Put the mask on and fasten it over the net.

● To make an Ice Maiden, drape silver foil film over the head, like the net, and place a silver or blue metallic card coronet over it.

HALLOWE'EN HAT

The Hallowe'en hat shown here can be personalized in many ways and can also be adapted for other purposes. Some of the ideas shown in other chapters could be used in conjunction with the hat.

Preparation

1. The hat is made in two parts – first the crown which is cone-shaped, and then the brim. Lay the sheet of black paper on a flat surface. Attach a piece of string to the pencil and make a mark on the string 18in/45cm from the point of the pencil. Place this mark in the corner of the paper and hold firmly. Position the point of the pencil on the edge of the paper so that the string is taut. Keeping the string under tension draw an arc to the other edge.

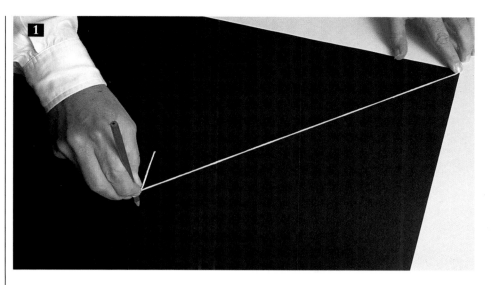

2. Cut out this shape, which is a quarter circle.

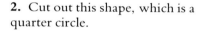

MATERIALS

- pencil and string

- scissors

- medium-weight black paper about 33in × 24in/85cm × 60cm

- clear adhesive and adhesive tape

- green and black crepe paper

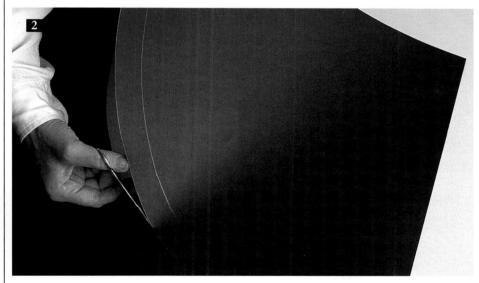

3. Now cut slits along the curved edge 1in/2cm deep. These will be used to stick the cone to the brim. Bend these tabs to the outside. Next curl the paper around on itself to form a cone. In order to make a neat finish, cut out a small square at the top. As heads vary in size, before the cone is fixed permanently, try it so that any adjustments can be made. The cone should be glued and then a little tape can be stuck inside for extra security.

TIPS

- An average head measures about 24in/60cm and a child's head a little less. In order that a child should not be dwarfed by the hat, mark the string at 16in/40cm and make the brim a little narrower.

- If the paper is too floppy for the brim, two circles can be cut at step 4 and the second can be glued to the underside of the hat, after the tabs have been stuck in place.

- This hat could be made in card of any colour and be used in conjunction with the hat masks, see page 98.

4. To make the brim, stand the cone in the middle of the remains of the sheet of black paper, with the tabs turned to the inside, and draw around the edge. Next decide on the width of the brim – 4in/10cm is average but it could be more or less, depending on the wearer and weight of the paper. The wider the brim the heavier the paper will need to be so that it does not flop down and hide the face. Draw a line the chosen width away from the first circle. Cut on both pencil lines and you will be left with a ring of paper.

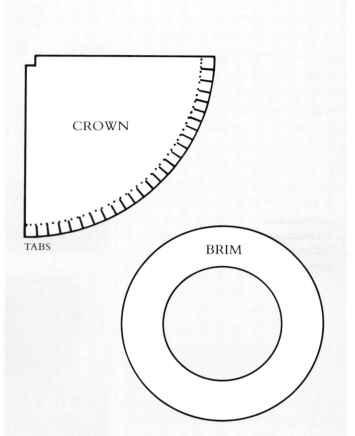

CROWN

TABS

BRIM

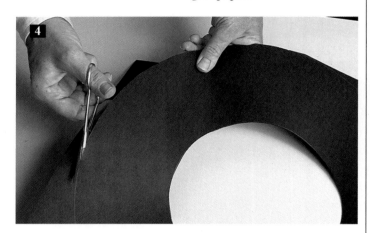

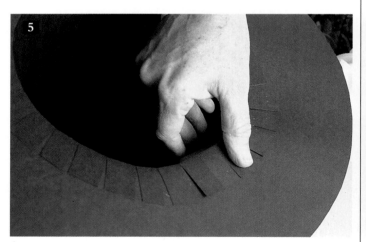

5. Push the cone through the hole in the centre of the brim so that the tabs, cut in step 2, are on the underside of the brim. Check that everything fits neatly and then, using the adhesive, stick the tabs in place on the brim.

6. To make the character more gruesome, hair can be added to the inside of the hat by cutting strips of the crepe paper and taping them inside the cone. Cut off a piece of each of the green and black crepe paper which will fit around half of the hat and is at least 16in/40cm long. Fold both pieces in half and put the black piece inside the green piece. Leaving a solid area of 1in/2cm at the top, cut narrow strips to represent hair and stick in place, using double-sided adhesive tape.

PAPIER-MÂCHÉ NOSE

This is a very simple shape to create and once you have made one you will probably want to experiment with lots of different shapes and sizes. A nose can be used on its own or with many different masks, as well as with a witch's hat.

Preparation

1. Create the basic shape of a nose using thick paper or card. You will probably need one piece for the bridge and one for the bottom of the nose. Join the pieces with masking tape.

2. Tear some newspaper into small pieces and dip them into the diluted adhesive (see instructions for papier mâché on page 89). Cover the nose shape evenly with several layers of newspaper. Try to make the final layer very smooth, covering the edges. Leave to dry thoroughly. If necessary sand any rough edges with fine sandpaper, then paint with white emulsion.

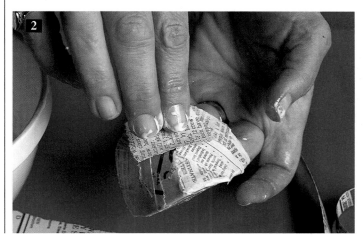

3. Having decided what kind of character the nose should represent, paint it to suit. When finished it could be varnished for durability. Hold the nose in place and decide where to make the holes for the elastic. Pierce carefully and thread the elastic through the holes and tie the knot.

MATERIALS

- pencil and scissors
- tracing paper
- medium-weight card
- masking tape
- old newspapers
- PVA adhesive
- white emulsion paint
- brush and paint
- elastic

FULL FACE MASKS

FULL FACE CARD MASKS

A card mask is the easiest full face mask to make. The simple shape can form the basis of numerous masks and it is not difficult to build up three dimensions from the flat surface.

ZEBRA

The template can be scaled up or down to fit the size of the wearer's head. Make it rather larger than the actual face as it will curve slightly when it is fastened.

MATERIALS

- basic face mask template page 119
- medium-weight white card same size as template
- pencil
- cutting knife
- black paint and thin brush
- black and white paper
- glue

Preparation

1. Draw round the template onto the card and cut out the shape. Cut out the eyes, nose and mouth. Draw in the zebra's stripes, in pencil, making them about 1⁄3in/1cm wide. Paint a thin black line around the eyes, nose and mouth. Paint in the stripes and leave to dry.

2. Make paper curls 1⁄4–1⁄2in/5–10mm wide in black and white paper (see techniques section, page 16).

3. Stick them to the top of the head. Use methods 1, 2 or 3 for fixing (see techniques section page 19).

MOUNTAIN MASK

Tibetan masks are a great source of inspiration for the following mask which should be very subtle in colour and materials.

MATERIALS

- basic face mask template page 119

- medium-weight dark green or dark blue card same size as template

- 14 white shirt buttons

- strip of maribou feathers – 15in/38cm long

- 10 oval cotton pulp shapes

- gold or bronze paint

- PVA glue

- craft knife

- scissors

Preparation

1. Draw round the template onto the card and cut out the shape. Cut out the eyes and mouth. Stick the buttons around the eyes.

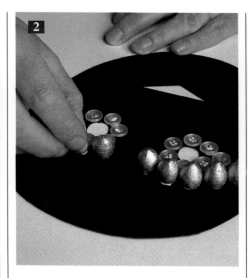

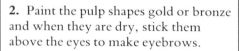

2. Paint the pulp shapes gold or bronze and when they are dry, stick them above the eyes to make eyebrows.

3. Cut the feather strip into 2 pieces, one 12in/30cm long and the other 3in/8cm long. Stick the shorter piece around the top of the head and the longer one around the bottom and sides of the face. Use method 1, 2 or 3 for fixing (see techniques section page 19).

FANTASY FULL FACE MASK

Preparation

1. Draw round the template onto the card and cut out the shape. Cut out the mouth. Change the eyes into diamonds, drawing the shapes first, then cut them out. Outline the eyes in black felt pen and stick the beads around them about ¼in/5mm from the edge.

2. Stick a line of 6 beads vertically, between the eyes for the nose and make a "v" shape of beads at the bottom for the nostrils.

3. Take a colour page from a magazine and cut random geometric shapes about ½in × ¾in/1cm × 2cm. Stick these around the bottom part of the mask to make a beard.

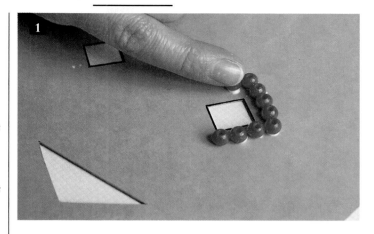

MATERIALS

- basic face mask template page 119

- medium-weight yellow ochre card same size as template

- 45 small red wooden beads ¼in/5mm in diameter

- colour pages from a magazine

- PVA glue

- craft knife

- black felt pen

- pencil and ruler

4. Make paper rolls (see techniques section page 16) out of another page.

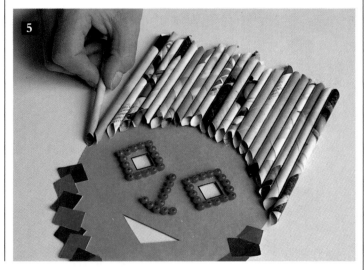

5. Make the rolls 4in–6in/10cm–15cm long and stick them across the top.

6. Make three rolls of the same colours – one 3in/7cm long and two 1½in/4cm long. Stick these around the mouth. Use method 1, 2 or 3 for fixing (see techniques section page 19).

RIDER MASK

This mask simulates the sixteenth- and seventeenth-century Italian rider's masks, which were worn to protect the face from branches when riding through wooded countryside. They were cut from thin sheets of metal and formed a type of armour. The designs could be quite decorative, however, and they inspired the simple cut-out mask below.

Preparation

1. Trace the basic mask shape. Either draw your own design or choose one of the rider mask patterns shown. If the mask is for an adult, take it to a photocopy shop and ask them to enlarge the pattern by 20 per cent. Trace the design onto the back of the foil card and then cut away the shaded areas with a craft knife. Make sure the work surface is protected either by a cutting mat or scrap card. Turn the mask over and smooth the cut edge where the knife may have caused a slight burr. If you are using white card this may not be necessary.

2. If you have made the mask from white card it should now be covered with the aluminium foil. Lay the foil over the mask and cut roughly to size allowing enough to turn over the edge. From the wrong side, cut a slit through each open area. Turn to the right side and bend all the edges to the back, making sure no excess shows. Hold the mask up to the face and mark the position of the holes for the elastic, string or ribbon. Pierce the holes, thread and tie.

MATERIALS

- basic face mask template page 119

- paper and pencil

- silver foil card or white card and aluminium foil 11in × 9in/ 28cm × 23cm

- craft knife

- elastic, string or ribbon

RIDER MASK TEMPLATE 1

TEMPLATE 2

TEMPLATE 3

ENLARGE TO 175% (INCREASE BY ¾)

ORIGAMI MASK

Quick and easy to make, the origami mask is extremely versatile. It can be made to represent many characters. In this example, the mask is decorated with paints and marker pens. As an alternative, the mask makes a very good bird.

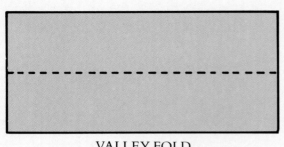

VALLEY FOLD

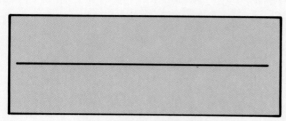

EXISTING CREASE

FOLD TOWARDS YOU

FOLD AWAY FROM YOU

MATERIALS

- pencil and ruler

- scissors or knife

- coloured paper

- hole punch and string

Preparation

1. Take paper measuring 12in/30cm square for a child and 14in/35cm square for an adult. As with all masks these measurements are adjustable for the individual. Fold and crease the paper diagonally and then flatten it before folding the two side corners to the previously creased centre line.

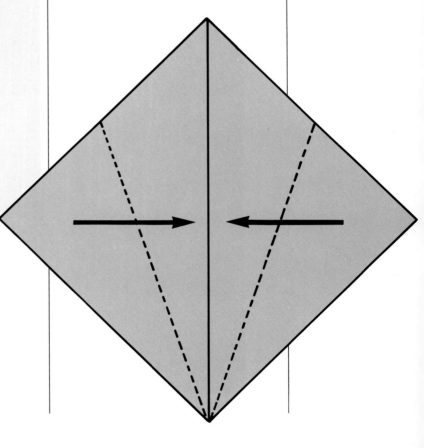

TIPS

- It is important to fold origami on a firm, flat surface such as the top of a table.

- If you have not done any origami before check that you understand the basic symbols shown on this page.

- Always make the fold crisply but do it slowly to ensure that you get the crease exactly where you want it to be.

- It may be a good idea to practise by folding a mask from a small square of paper first, before starting on the actual mask.

2. The paper now looks like this.

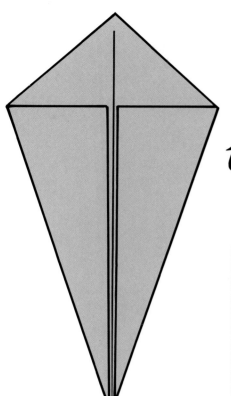

4. Fold the paper (including the point) towards the back along the previously creased centre line.

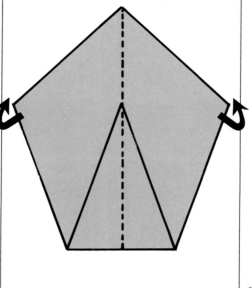

5. Now pull the point forward and crease at a suitable angle to represent a beak or a nose.

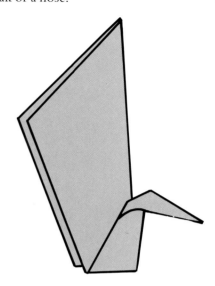

6. Cut out appropriate holes for the eyes and decorate as you like. Make small holes at the widest point and attach the ties. Fixing methods 1, 2 or 3 would be suitable for this mask.

3. Turn the paper over and fold the bottom point up to a point on the centre line at the widest part of the folded paper.

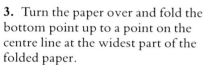

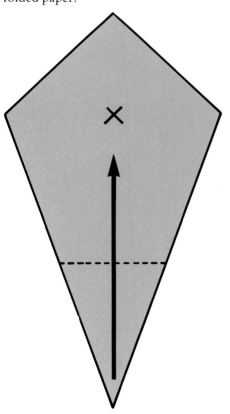

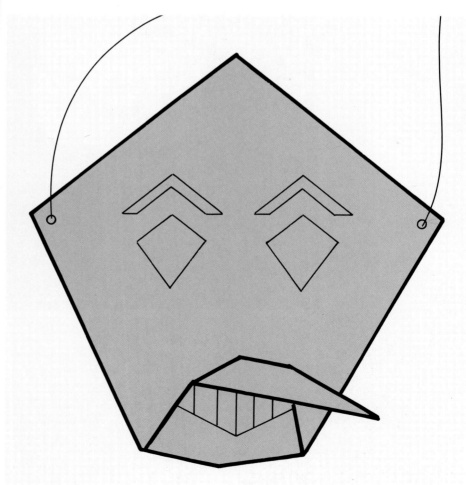

DRAGON

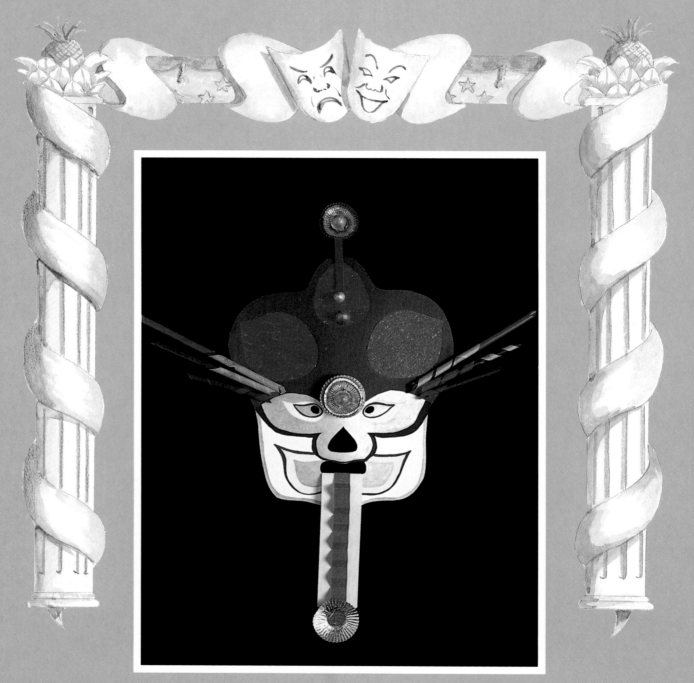

A very important symbol in all parts of Asia, especially China, Hong
Kong, Tibet, Sri Lanka and Indonesia, the dragon is a colourful and crucial
element in many celebrations and festivals. Often the dragon is made into a
large whole-head mask, sometimes with a large mouth, articulated jaws,
huge bulbous eyes and a large mane of coloured hair.

This dragon is a flat mask and is very simple to make. It can be as ornate and decorative as you want depending on the materials you have available. The mask can be made to wear on the face or attached to a stick to wave in front of the face when appropriate.

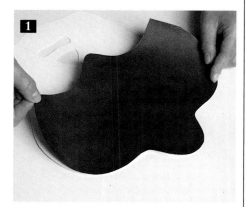

MATERIALS

- dragon template page 120

- medium-weight white card 14in × 12in/35cm × 30cm

- black or dark coloured paper 12in × 8in/30cm × 20cm

- coloured papers in 2 lengths of contrasting colours 2in × 12in/ 5cm × 30cm

- gold or silver metallic marker

- paints and thin brush

- pulp shapes

- lollipop sticks

- coloured translucent paper or tissue paper

- coloured crinkle foil paper

- various metallic and coloured fondant cases

- PVA glue

- pencil

- craft knife

Preparation

1. Draw round the template onto the white card and cut it out. Draw round the head-dress area onto the black or dark coloured paper and cut it out. Stick this shape onto the white card.

2. Draw in the facial features with silver or gold metallic markers. Make the eyes and mouth big and bold.

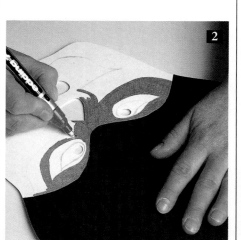

3. Add the final details of the face with red and black paint.

4. When decorating the head dress stick lots of brightly coloured materials onto the black paper area. Do not be afraid of having lots of different colours and textures, but do aim for some symmetry to avoid ending up with a mess. Cut out three bright shapes from the crinkle foil and stick them onto the head-dress.

5. Add painted or natural lollipop sticks, and stick painted pulp shapes, fondant cases or scrunched tissue paper (see techniques section page 18) onto them. Stick these to the top of the head-dress. Make paper rolls (see techniques section page 18) out of translucent paper or tissue paper and stick these to the sides.

6. Make the tongue by taking a strip of coloured paper 2in × 8in/5cm × 20cm (or longer if you want). Fold over one end and make a point at the other. Take a piece of paper ¾in × 12in/ 2cm × 30cm in a contrasting colour and pleat it, making each pleat about ½in/1½cm side. (See techniques section page 18.) Put a little glue on alternate concertina fold edges and stick it down the middle of the previous long strip of paper.

7. Hook the folded end of the tongue into the dragon's mouth and stick with tape, from behind. Stick a metallic fondant case or other decoration to the bottom of the tongue. This forms a basic tongue but you could always add further decoration to it. For fastening use method 5 or 4A (see techniques section 19).

TIP

■ The wearer's nose could be painted a colour – white or deep red (see face paints section page 32).

THE SUN AND MOON

*These extended full face masks of the sun and moon are made out of flat card
and complement the Four Seasons masks.*

MOON

Preparation

1. Draw round the template onto the card and cut out the moon shape. Cut out the eyes, nose and mouth. Draw in the arc to make the crescent. Scrunch (see techniques section page 16) and tear tissue paper and doilies and stick onto the crescent shape of the card to make a rich, but not too thick, textured surface. Try to keep the curve of the crescent arc.

MATERIALS

- sun and crescent moon template page 121

- medium-weight white card 12in/30cm square

- white paper doilies

- white tissue paper

- silver and gold glitter

- silver spray paint

- dark blue and black paint

- paint brush

- gold and silver star shaped stickers

- glue

- pencil

- craft knife and scissors

2. Spray the crescent with silver paint.

3. Paint the rest of the card dark blue/black for the night and when dry put the star stickers on. Use method 5 for fixing (see techniques section page 19).

SUN

Preparation

1. Draw round the template onto the white card and cut out the sun shape. Cut out the features as for the moon. Make a collage on the sun's face, as in the moon mask (step 2 in the previous project), using the yellow tissue paper. Outline the smiling eyes and mouth with a thin row of scrunched, orange tissue paper. Carefully arrange the yellow tissue paper so that it covers the nose.

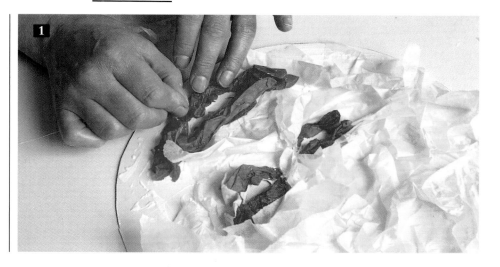

2. Gently spray with a thin layer of gold paint, retaining some of the yellow and orange colour beneath.

3. Trim round the edge of the face.

MATERIALS

- sun and crescent moon template page 121

- medium-weight white card 12in/30cm square

- medium-weight white card 8in × 24in/20cm × 60cm

- gold crinkle foil paper 8in × 24in/20cm × 60cm

- pale yellow and light orange tissue paper

- gold spray paint

- pencil

- craft knife and scissors

- glue and adhesive tape

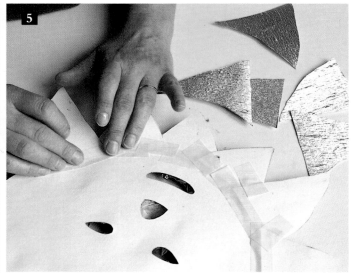

4. Cut out the sun rays in white card, three of the smallest shape and six each of the larger shapes. Cover the sun rays with gold crinkle foil paper.

5. Place the smallest three rays at the bottom of the face and tape from behind. They should slightly overlap and be taped to each other as well as to the card. Repeat this process around the sun with the other rays, alternating their shapes. By overlapping they will support each other and not flop when in position. Use method 5 for fixing (see techniques section page 19).

TIP

You could use this sun as a basic shape and paint it with orange, yellow and gold paints.

AMERICAN INDIAN MASK

This style lends itself very nicely to the shape created by a papier-mâché balloon mask. Traditionally carved from wood, the mask images are usually taken from animal forms. American Indians lived in harmony with nature and their folklore gave equality to all living things. Although they recognized that their physical appearances differed from animals, they felt they were descended from them and each tribe had a special affinity with a particular animal such as a bear, a wolf or an eagle. It is for this reason that many of their carvings take on the appearance of half animal, half man.

Preparation

1. Blow up the balloon so that when it is held in front of you it is impossible to see the face. Tie firmly with string and cover with a thin coating of the release agent. One balloon will make two masks. Dilute the PVA with water to the consistency of thin cream and tear the newspaper into strips about 1in/3cm wide. Make sure your working area is protected as the next stage may be a little messy. Cover the balloon with the first layer of paper. If the balloon jumps around a bit hold it in place on top of a bowl.

MATERIALS

- medium-weight card
- balloon and string
- release agent (petroleum jelly)
- old newspapers
- PVA adhesive
- tracing paper and card
- pencil
- craft knife and scissors
- sandpaper
- emulsion paint
- paint brushes
- paints
- varnish

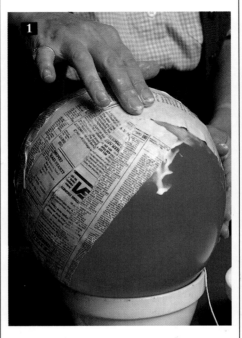

3. Make the beak shape next. Cut two side pieces and one base piece from medium-weight card. Stick these pieces together with masking tape and cover with several layers of PVA-soaked newspaper strips. It will be necessary to use quite small strips in order to cover the shape smoothly. Leave both balloon and beak to dry for 24 hours.

2. Put on second layer – try to use paper of a different colour to make it easier to see what you are doing. Continue in this way until you have completed eight layers. Try to make the last layer especially smooth to save time and work later.

4. Now cut the papier-mâché balloon in half. It is easier if you draw a line around the balloon first and then cut carefully on the line with a craft knife, using a sawing action. The balloon may pop or it may just stick to the inside of the mould but it will peel away easily.

5. Put on some lipstick and place the mask in front of your face. When it feels as if it is sitting comfortably, press your lips to the inside of the mask so that the lipstick marks the position of the mouth. Draw the required mouth shape on the inside and cut this out. On your own face, measure up from the mouth to the bridge of the nose and mark this distance on the mask. Now measure the distance between the centres of your eyes. Mark the position of the eyes on the papier-mâché. Draw in the shape of the eyes and cut them out carefully.

6. Take the beak shape and trim the open edges. Using masking tape, stick the beak in position on the mask. Now take some newspaper strips and diluted PVA adhesive and cover the join with two or three layers of paper.

7. Trim the edge of the mask and then bind all the cut edges – outer, mouth and eyes – with small pieces of newspaper. Leave to dry again. Paint the whole mask white.

8. Next draw the outline of the final design on to the surface of the mask. Mix the coloured paints to a smooth consistency and paint carefully. Allow the paint to dry overnight and then varnish. Make holes in the sides of the mask slightly above eye level and thread string or ribbon through the holes so that the mask can be tied in place.

WHOLE HEAD MASKS

BAG PEOPLE

*Paper bag people are very easy and quick to make. The more varied your
paper bags the more interesting the crowd will be.*

Preparation

1. Try the bag on the head and make sure it fits. Pull it well down and carefully pencil in the eyes and mouth positions. Take the bag off and lay it down. Using the basic face template draw in the shapes of the eyes and mouth over your pencil marks. Put the piece of heavy-weight card inside the bag to make a cutting surface. Cut out the eyes and mouth. Paint in the details of the lips, cheeks and eyebrows. You can add cheeks and wrinkles if you want as well!

2. Make hair out of lots of thin coloured ribbon and stick it all over. Alternatively you could make hair out of coloured cartridge paper cut into fine strips, some curled (see page 16) and some straight and stuck on like the lion on page 102. Coloured tissue and crepe papers can be cut into strips, some with straight edges and others zigzagged with pinking shears. Paper doilies can also be used. A variety of different hairstyles will quickly appear.

MATERIALS

- large paper bag about 12in × 16in/30cm × 40cm (check that it fits)

- basic face template page 119

- piece of heavy-weight card slightly smaller than the bag

- craft knife

- PVA glue

- red and black paints and brushes

- decorative materials such as thin ribbon, crepe paper, tissue paper and cartridge paper strips

SAFETY

Use only paper bags, not plastic or polythene bags, which are very dangerous because they may cause suffocation. If you have any doubts about the bag you have chosen, do not use it.

KNITTED FACE-MASK

This mask can be used on its own or in conjunction with an eye mask for total anonymity. The knitted face-mask or balaclava, originally used by soldiers on active service in the second half of the 19th century, was a woollen covering for the head and shoulders. It was probably designed for purely practical reasons during the Crimean War at the Battle of Balaklava, where the cold was bitter. A similar type of head covering can be seen in the Bayeux Tapestry, where it appears to be made from chainmail. Several tribes in Mexico and Peru use balaclava-type masks as face protection against the weather.

The version used here covers more of the face than a normal balaclava as the intention of a burglar would be total disguise. This mask can be adapted for different characters such as the cat shown below, which has been made from bits of wool and has had ears added. A very simple mask can be made from a tube of stockinette jersey material sewn across the top and with a slit cut for the eyes.

MATERIALS

■ Two 3oz/50g balls black double knitting wool

■ pair each of needles size 10/3¼mm and 8/4mm

■ wool needle for sewing up

Abbreviations

k – knit; p – purl; st(s) – stitch(es); st.st. – stocking stitch; tog – together; tbl – through back of loop; dec – decrease; inc – increase; alt – alternate.

Preparation

Using 3¼mm needles, cast on 98sts.
Work 26 rows in k1, p1, rib.
Change to 4mm needles.
Work 2 rows in st. st.
Next row: k39, k2tog, k16, k2tog tbl, k to end.
Next row: Purl.
Next row: k38, k2tog, k16, k2tog tb1, k to end. (94sts).
Continue in st.st. for a further 13 rows.
Next row: work to last 10sts, leave these on a safety pin.
Repeat this row once. (74sts remain on the needle.)
Dec 1st at each end of next 2 alt. rows. (70sts).
Work straight in st.st. for 19 rows.
Inc. 1st at each end of next 5 alt. rows. (80sts)
Work 1 row.
Cast on 11sts at end of next 2 rows. (102)sts.
Next row: (k1, k2tog, k20, k2tog tbl) twice, k2tog, (k2tog, k20, k2tog tb1, k1) twice. (93sts)
Next and following alt. rows: purl.
Next row: k1, k2tog (k18, k2tog tb1, k1p1, k2tog) 3 times, k18, k2tog tb1,

k1p1. (85sts)
Next dec row: k1, k2tog (k16, k2tog tb1, k1, k2tog) 3 times, k16, k2tog tb1, k1. (77sts)
Next dec row has 14 sts between decreases.
Next dec row has 12 sts between decreases.
Continue in this manner until 13sts remain.
Purl 1 row.

Next row: k1 (k2tog, k1) 4 times. (9sts)
Break yarn and thread through remaining sts, draw up and fasten off.
Sew up head seam using wool needle.
Using 10/3¼mm needles with right side of work facing, pick up and knit 78sts evenly along face edge including the sts. previously left on safety pins.
Work 7 rows in k1, p1, rib. Cast off in rib.
Sew up neck seam.

TIP

■ You can create a cat by adding knitted or fabric ears to the mask Then use face paints to make a nose and whiskers. You can also make the whiskers from paper.

HAT MASKS

A hat can be used to make a whole head mask with lots of long straggly hair. The Zambians make a woven straw hat with a face piece of the same material attached to the front. There are many ways in which you can make hat masks and here are two examples. The possibilities for variations are numerous and you will want to use your own ideas to adapt and change these masks.

NATURAL HAT MASK

Preparation

1. Measure the inside of the hat and cut a piece of linen tape to that length plus 1in/1.5cm. Lay the muslin out, make sure it is not creased. Place the face template over it, about 6in/15cm from the top. Pencil in the outline of the eyes and mouth. Remove template and paint in the outlines with fabric paints or crayons. Leave to dry.

2. Lay out the linen tape. Put glue along a stretch of tape the same length as the top of the muslin face piece. Stick the tape onto the right side of the muslin and press well down. Turn the tape and face piece over.

MATERIALS

- straw hat

- white muslin or net 9in × 14in/23cm × 35cm

- basic face mask template page 119

- natural coloured raffia

- wooden beads (optional)

- ½in/1cm wide linen tape – 5ft/1.5m long

- fabric paints or crayons

- PVA glue

- stapler (optional)

- masking tape

- needle and thread

- pencil

- scissors

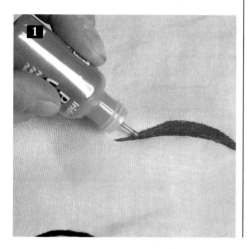

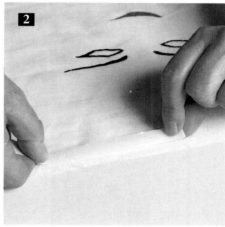

3. Cut lengths of raffia about 18in/45cm long. It is best to stick the raffia to the tape in stages – about 8in/20cm of tape at a time. Put a little glue onto the tape and stick the end part of a bunch of raffia to it and press it firmly down. When sticking the raffia in place make sure some of it overlaps the edge of the muslin face piece. You might need to hold the raffia and tape in place with masking tape in order to make it really secure.

4. Spread more glue on top of the linen tape and raffia when the entire length has been covered. Cut another piece of linen tape, the same length as the original and put it on top of the raffia and muslin. Press down hard and leave to dry. You might like to staple the raffia in place, through the fabric tape to give extra strength.

5. Lay the raffia wig and the face on the inside of the hat, making sure the face is at the front. Use masking tape to hold in place. Now stitch into place with needle and thread.

Try the mask on. You can cut the raffia hair shorter and thread wooden beads into it if you want. If the stitching and tape show through, the top of the hat and the sides can be decorated with a hat band of raffia.

TIPS

■ You could make the carnival mask without the muslin face and make the wig go all the way round the head. Or you could paint the wearer's face (see face painting page 32).

■ If you are unable to find a straw hat make the Hallowe'en hat (see page 64) in an appropriately coloured card and stick the wig to the inside of it.

CARNIVAL HAT MASK

Preparation

1. Make this wig in the same way as the natural mask above following steps 1–5. At step 1 paint the face in bright colours. At step 3 use the ribbons, tapes and string to make a mixed wig. Or you could make a wig using thin strips of different coloured crepe paper.

2. Thread a selection of beads and buttons into the hair. If the stitching and linen tape show through, then you can decorate the hat with a hat band of different ribbons, string and beads.

MATERIALS

- straw hat

- white muslin or net 9in × 14in/ 23cm × 35cm

- basic face mask template see page 119

- selection of coloured ribbons, fabric tapes, foil tapes, coloured string for the hair

- crepe paper (optional)

- wooden and plastic beads, buttons in lots of colours (optional)

- 1¼in/3cm wide linen tape 5ft/ 1.5m long

- fabric paints or crayons

- double-sided tape

- masking tape

- PVA glue

- stapler (optional)

- needle and thread

- pencil

- scissors

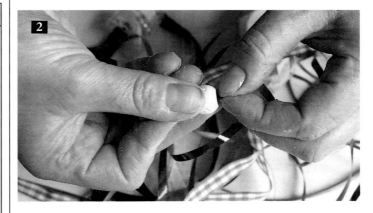

LEO THE LION

Children love to roar behind this full head lion mask. Easy to make from flat card, the lion becomes three-dimensional at the very end. It can be adjusted to fit various head sizes.

Preparation

1. Lay out the large sheet of beige card horizontally. Draw a light pencil line down the middle of the card from top to bottom. Having enlarged the main part of the template lay it over the card so that the pencil line is half-way between the eyes. Draw round the features. Cut out the eyes and mouth and make the ear slits.

MATERIALS

- whole head lion template see page 112

- light-weight beige or light brown card 28in × 11in/70cm × 28cm (the grain running down the shorter side)

- another shade of brown card 4in × 12in/10cm × 30cm

- light-weight white card 5in × 4in/12cm × 10cm

- coloured paper in black, beige and white

- brown and pink paint and brushes

- adhesive tape

- glue

- paper clips

- craft knife and scissors

- pencil and ruler

2. Place the chin template on the white card and the ears and nose on the brown card. Draw round them and cut them out. Score (see techniques page 17) the sides of the nose along the line indicated on the template. Carefully bend them back to make flaps. Apply glue to the flaps and stick them in place.

3. Gently push the sides towards each other so that the bridge of the nose is slightly raised.

4. Slot the ears into the ear slots and hold them in place with tape on the back of the card.

TIP

This method of mask making can be used to make many other animals. To design your own mask find a photograph of the animal you choose and make a large drawing of its most important features. Superimpose the tube shape onto this, then trace off the features and you will have the basis of the new mask.

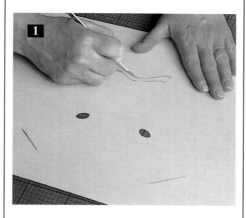

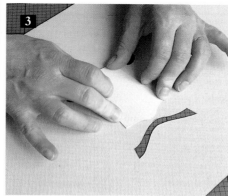

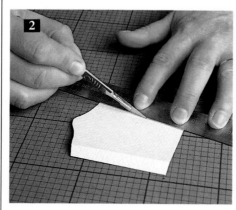

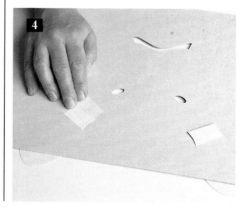

5. Make the hair with the three coloured papers. You will need lots of hair in various lengths and thicknesses – a lion can be quite unkempt! Take a piece of paper, score and fold a line about ½in/1cm from the left edge to make the sticking strip. Cut strips between ⅛in-¼in/ 3mm-7mm wide across the paper from the fold. Curl the thicker strips (see techniques section page 16).

6. Make short white straight hair and stick it onto the chin. Fold back the sticking strip so that it is hidden beneath the hair. Apply glue to the side away from the hair. Stick the chin onto the lion.

7. Accentuate the facial features with the paint. He might need a pink nose and lines around the eyes.

8. Attach the rest of the hair to the lion. Put short pieces along the top of the head and longer pieces down the side of the face. Make the very long pieces go right over the top of the head and down the back. Add some shorter pieces to the back if required.

9. Bend the mask around the head of the wearer and fasten it into shape with paper clips at the top or bottom. Take it off and stand it on the table. You can staple the back of the head in place or, if the mask is to be used by different people use the paper clips so that the fastening can vary according to the size of the head.

HORSE HEAD MASK

The stylized horse head has been turned into a mask by using very simple paper engineering techniques. As with other designs in the book, when creating this design the basic characteristics of the horse have been closely observed and incorporated into the pattern. All the lines have been simplified and other animals can be created in this way – particular attention should be paid to ears, the width of the head and the nose. The eyes will need great care – in this example it has not been possible to cut the eye holes in the right place so small holes have been pierced to suit the wearer.

Preparation

1. Trace the pattern from the template section and enlarge. Draw the pattern onto the wrong side of the brown card and cut out, taking particular care when cutting around the ears and the tabs.

2. Now mark all the lines to be scored and the position of the slots for the tabs. This can be done at each end of the slot by piercing the card with a pin or similar sharp instrument. Score all the lines – if the card is very thick it will be necessary to cut through part of the card – see techniques section page 17. On the head part, gently bend the curve between the ears. Bend the side pieces from the outer edge of the ear to the nose and also the neck edge to the outer ear. The scored line from the inner edge of the ear to the nose should only be gently creased to give additional shaping to the mask. On the neck part of the mask bend all the scored lines.

3. Check that the position of the slots is correct by aligning the mask parts, adjust as necessary. Then cut the slots. If the card is thick it will be necessary to cut out a thin sliver of card. It is better that the slot should be tight as it can always be enlarged. Now cut out the eyes as indicated on the template – note that a very small area has been cut away. Score the small curved lines and bend the two parts to the inside. Hold the two cut edges together with a piece of adhesive tape on the wrong side. Assemble the two parts – head and neck. Slot head sides together and then the head top. On the neck part work from the top, being careful to align the lower tab before pushing the upper tab into position. Now join the two parts, making sure that the tabs slot in firmly.

4. Cut a strip of fur fabric for the mane, which will fit from the top of the head to the bottom of the neck. Fold in a very narrow turning and glue this down – it will make the edge of the fur fabric stand up in a most realistic way. Apply glue down the centre of the neck from the top of the head and stick on the "mane". Hold in place until the glue dries.

Cut another piece of fur fabric to positon between the ears and, using the same method, stick it in place. This piece may require some hairdressing! If fur fabric is not available, use various papers, such as thin coloured, crepe and translucent papers, stuck in layers and cut into narrow strips. This is the same method described in greater detail on page 102 for the Lion mask.

5. Finally pierce the two holes marked on the lower jaw and thread the elastic through these holes. Tie so that the jaw is held in and looks horse-like rather than cow-like! If it is difficult to see through the horse's eyes, extra eye holes can be pierced.

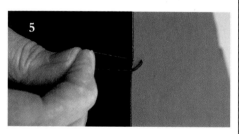

MATERIALS

■ horse head template, page 124

■ two sheets brown card (minimum size 24in × 16½in/ 60cm × 42cm)

■ pencil and ruler

■ craft knife and scissors

■ cutting mat or scrap card

■ bone folder (if available)

■ fur fabric of a suitable colour or light-weight papers

■ elastic

ASTRONAUT MASK

This mask has a very simple shape but takes quite a long time to make as it is constructed in two halves. The decoration is quite straightforward and the materials required are readily obtainable. It will be necessary to refer to the American Indian Mask in the previous chapter, see page 89 for detailed instructions on papier-mâché making. In this chapter one very simple method of making a mould will be explained. There are other ways and, it is hoped, you will wish to investigate them.

The mould has been made by piling screwed-up newspaper onto a flat polythene-covered board and taping the pieces so that they stay in position. The shape into which the newspaper pieces are placed is decided by taking a few basic measurements – overall height, width and depth. If there are any curves, look carefully where these occur and use the tape to create the right shape.

When you are satisfied that the overall appearance is correct, cover the mould with polythene – this will provide a smooth surface on which to lay the strips. Put a thin layer of petroleum jelly over the surface, then you are ready to start putting on the newspaper strips. The first layer may be a little awkward but if you use long strips it will help. Making the second layer go in the opposite direction will help you to keep the layers even and will add to the strength.

Preparation
1. As the mask sits on the shoulders, it will be necessary to measure from the shoulder to the top of the head to ascertain the height measurement. The width is measured across from ear to ear. When working out the depth measurement be sure to remember that you should halve it, as the mask is made in two halves. The depth is measured from the back of the head to the front. All the measurements should be generous as the finished mask has no openings and simply slips over the head of the wearer.

Roughly mark out the dimensions on the board and start piling up the newspapers. Do not try to make a cube – the head is rounded! As the pile grows it may be necessary to tape it down as you go along. When you are satisfied with the shape, cover it with polythene – some old plastic bags will serve the purpose.

MATERIALS

- polythene- or plastic-covered base board for the mould
- old newspapers
- sheet of thin polythene or plastic
- masking tape
- petroleum jelly or similar for release agent
- PVA adhesive
- thick string
- pencil
- sheet of thin acetate for visor
- sandpaper
- white paint

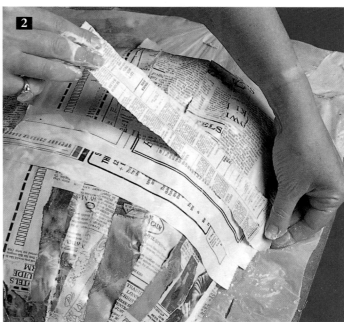

2. Using long strips of newspaper, cover the mould right down on to the base board. Continue to build up the layers until eight layers have been completed. Leave in a warm place to dry out thoroughly.

3. Carefully lift the half mask off the mould and set aside until you have completed the second half. Do not worry if the two halves are not absolutely identical.

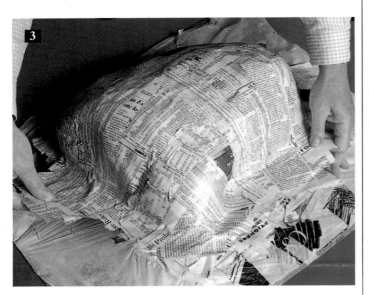

4. Cut away the edge of the mask, which was on the base board, including the neck area, and then hold the two halves together to see how well they fit. If necessary, trim away extra bits until the halves touch all round, as much as possible. Small gaps can be covered when the two pieces of the mask are joined.

5. Now cut out the window for the visor in one of the halves. This should be almost as wide as the face and from mid-forehead to mid-chin.

6. Tape the two halves together and carefully try on the mask. Join with three or four layers of newspaper strips. At the same time bind all the cut edges. Leave to dry.

7. Cut the acetate so that it overlaps the window by ½in/1cm and stick it in place with small pieces of masking tape and newspaper.

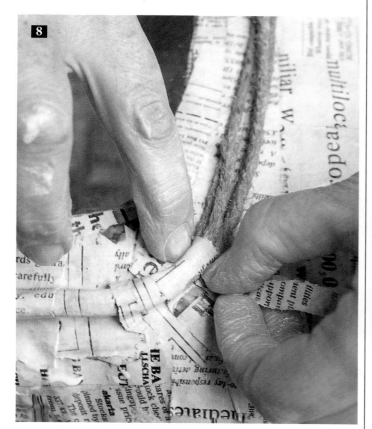

8. Make a border round the window with string covered by two or three layers of papier-mâché.

9. Use sandpaper to smooth away any noticeable bumps, which may have occurred particularly around the join.

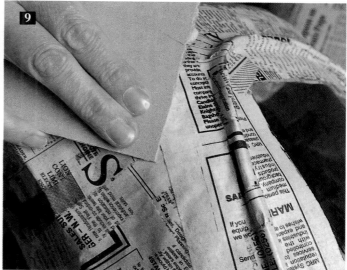

10. Paint with two coats of emulsion, carefully avoiding the visor area.

TEMPLATES

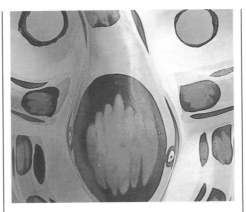

These templates are to be used as the basis for the mask patterns in the project section of the book. They are all labelled and have page references so that you will know which is which.

As every face is different it is not possible to give a universal pattern for every style of mask so you will have to tailor the mask to fit your needs. A good fitting mask should feel comfortable and the wearer should be able to see through the eye holes without difficulty. With an eye mask, for instance, the position of the wearer's cheek bones will influence the depth of the mask. Some people have eyes wide apart and others have a pronounced bridge to the nose. You should be aware of these when tailoring the mask to fit.

In the first instance it is suggested that you trace the pattern on to paper or thin card and try it on the face. Cut or extend this basic shape where necessary and in this way you will be able to personalize the patterns. You will soon become accomplished at altering where necessary.

Some of the templates are not shown full size. Any alterations to these will need to be made after the pattern has been enlarged. There are two methods of enlarging patterns.

The smaller patterns can be blown up on a photocopier. In some instances the instructions will tell you by what percentage the pattern should be increased. Otherwise you could ask the advice of the operator of the photocopier.

The second and more time-consuming method of enlarging patterns is by using a grid system. Trace off the pattern you wish to enlarge and draw a frame closely around it. Divide this frame into a number of small squares. On another piece of tracing paper draw another frame, which will be big enough to contain the enlarged pattern. Divide this second frame into the same number of squares as the first frame with the pattern. Now, transfer the pattern to the second frame by methodically marking points on the grid as the lines from the pattern cross over the squares. Finally join all the marks and the pattern will be ready.

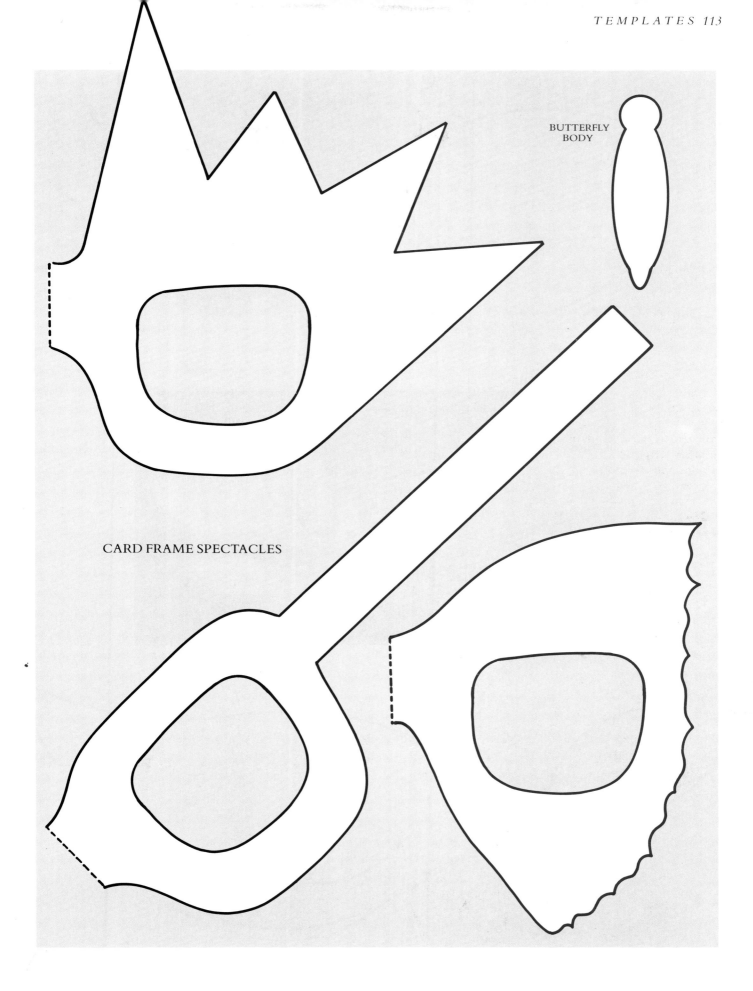

BUTTERFLY
BODY

CARD FRAME SPECTACLES

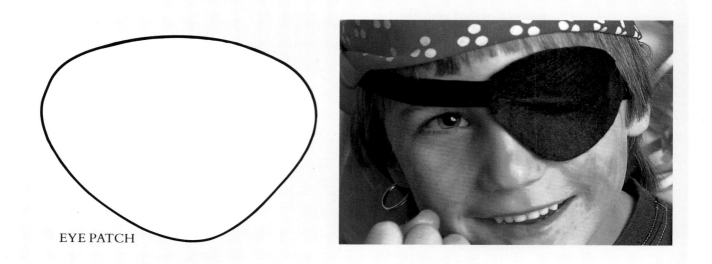

EYE PATCH

EYE MASK 3

EYE MASK 1

EYE MASK 2

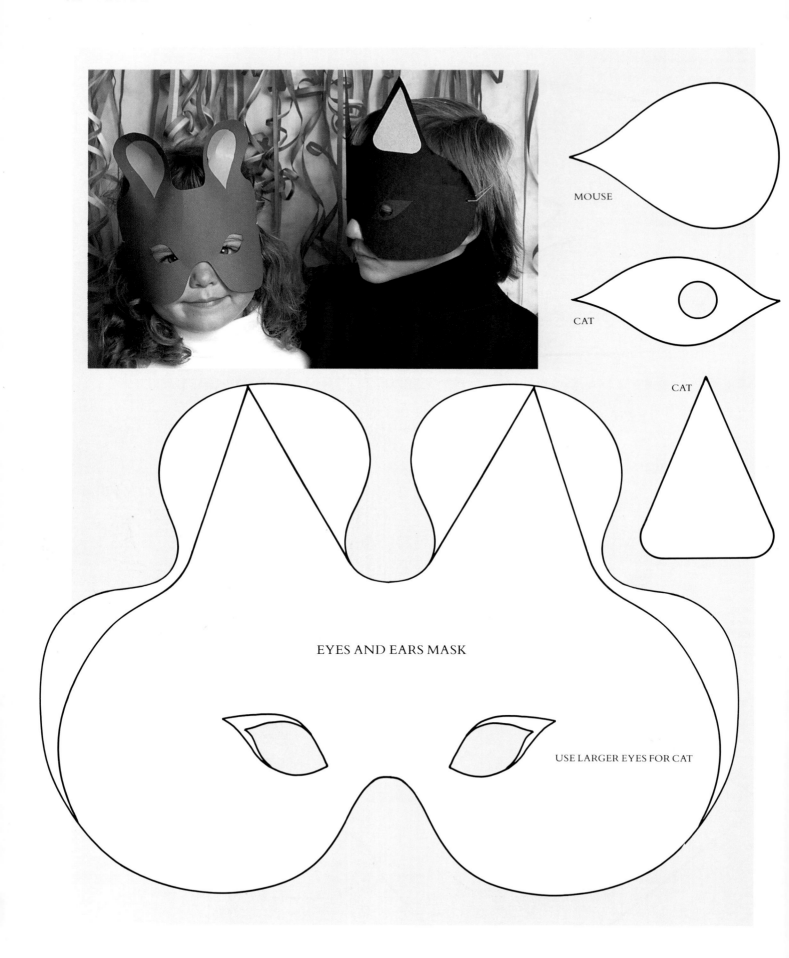

MOUSE

CAT

CAT

EYES AND EARS MASK

USE LARGER EYES FOR CAT

CROWNS AND CORONETS

HARLEQUIN

BASIC FACE MASK

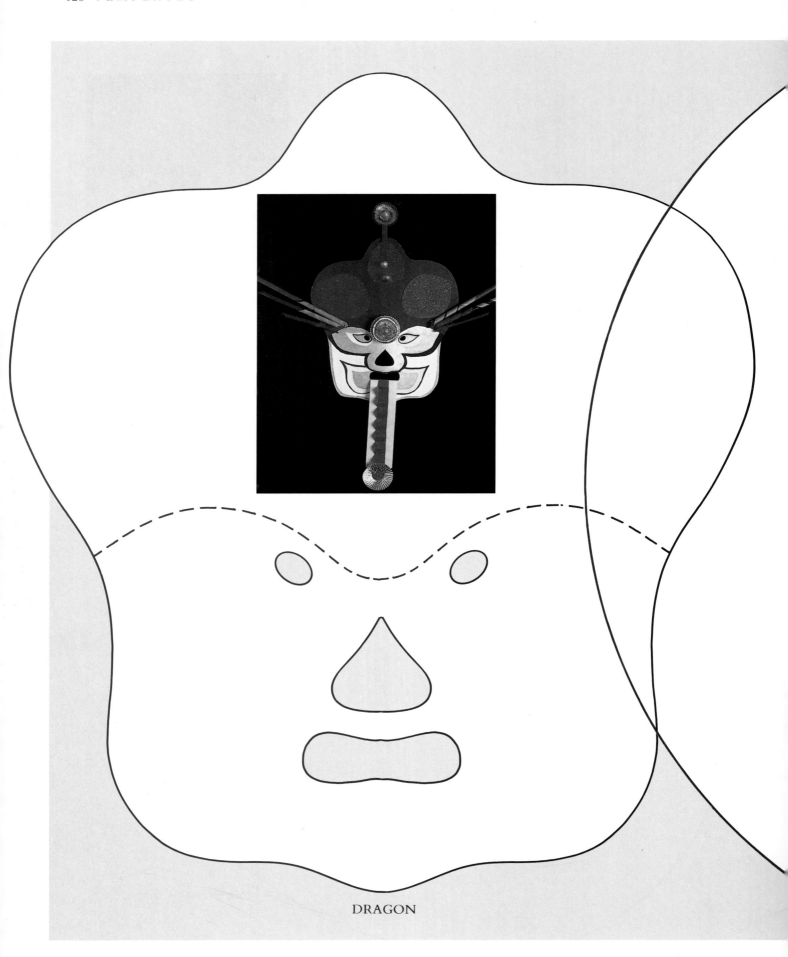

DRAGON

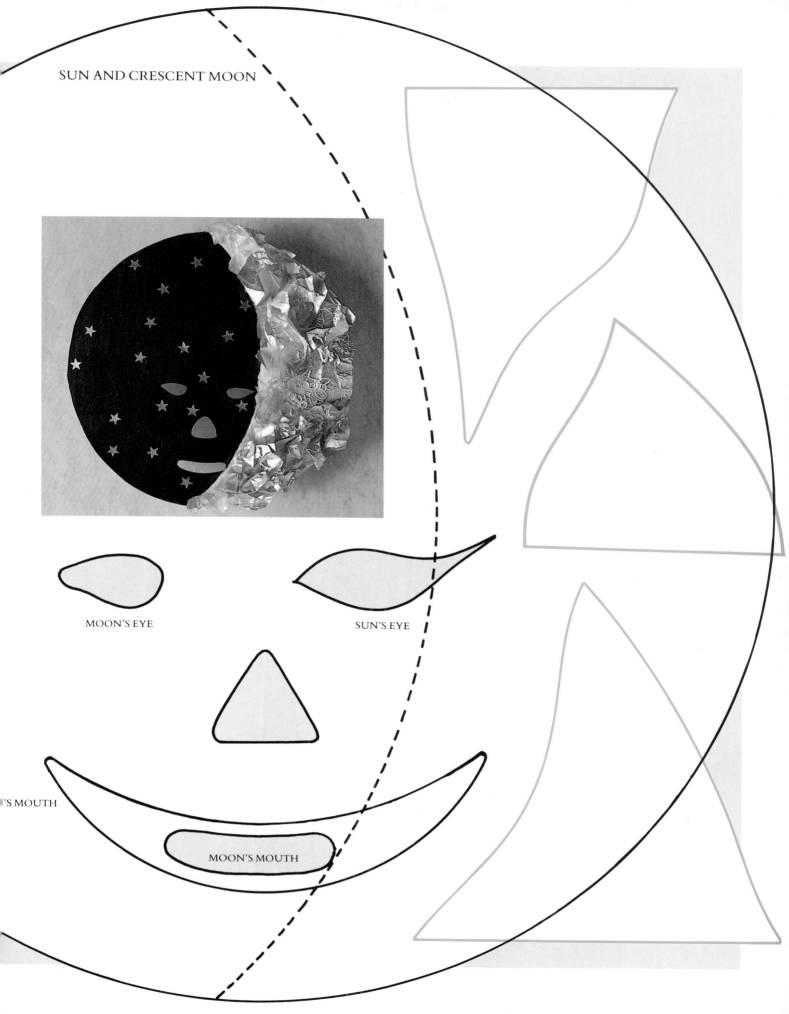

SUN AND CRESCENT MOON

MOON'S EYE

SUN'S EYE

MOON'S MOUTH

T'S MOUTH

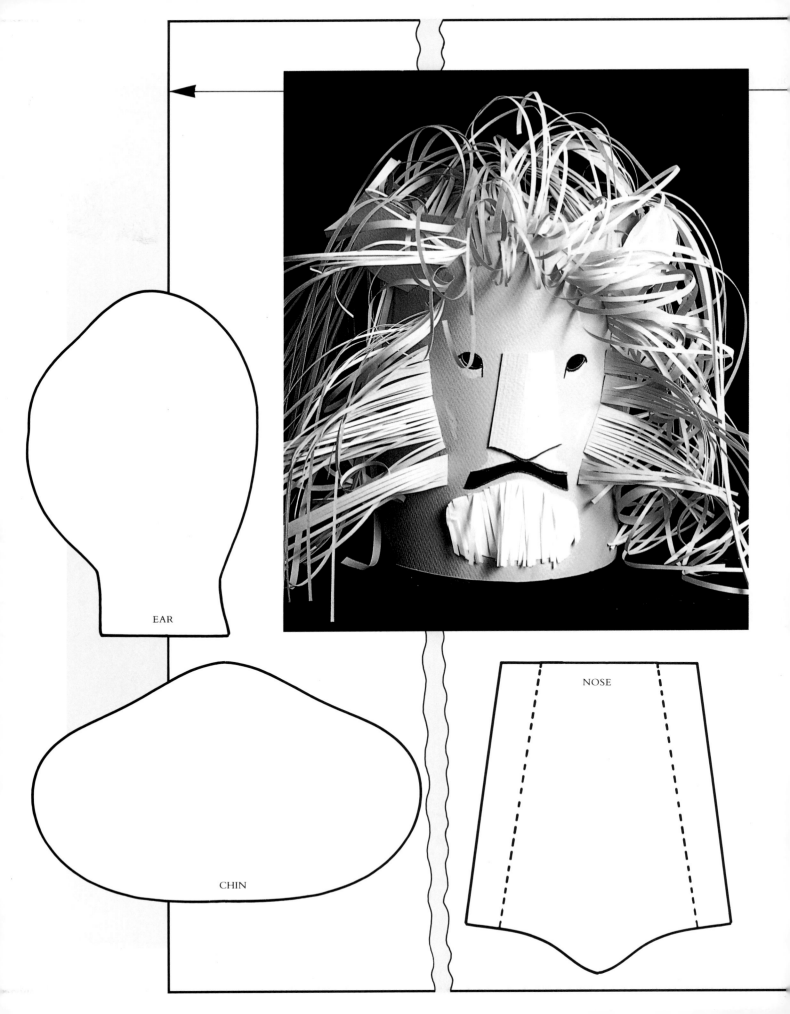

EAR

CHIN

NOSE

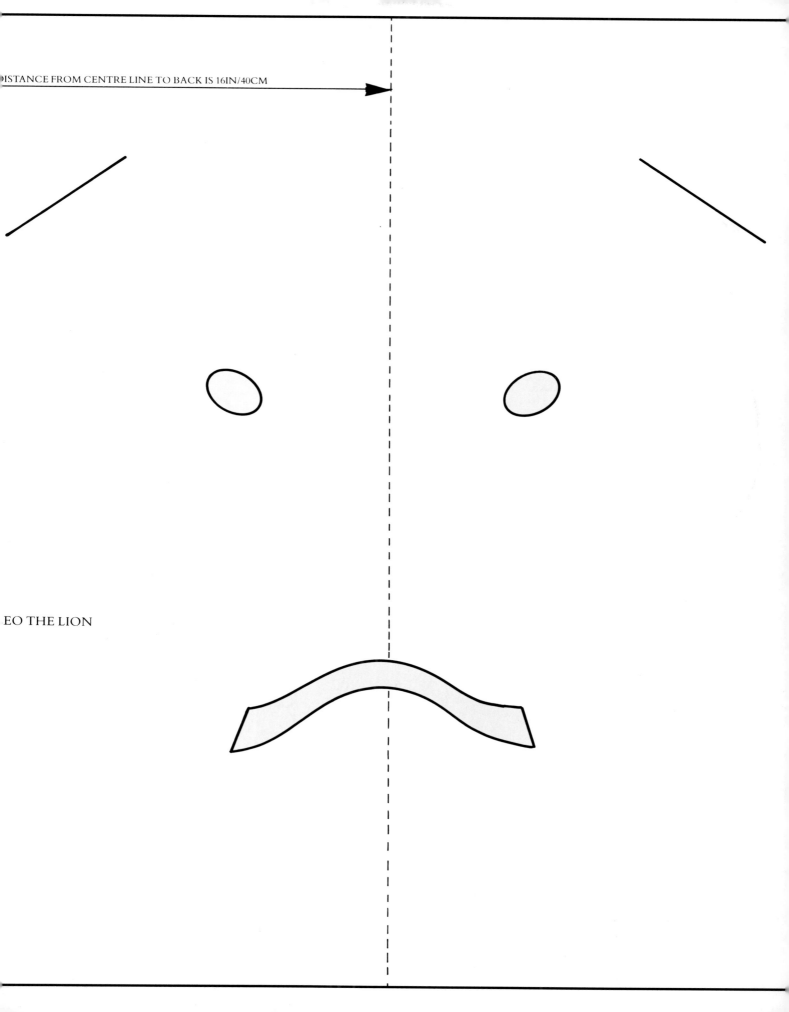

DISTANCE FROM CENTRE LINE TO BACK IS 16IN/40CM

EO THE LION

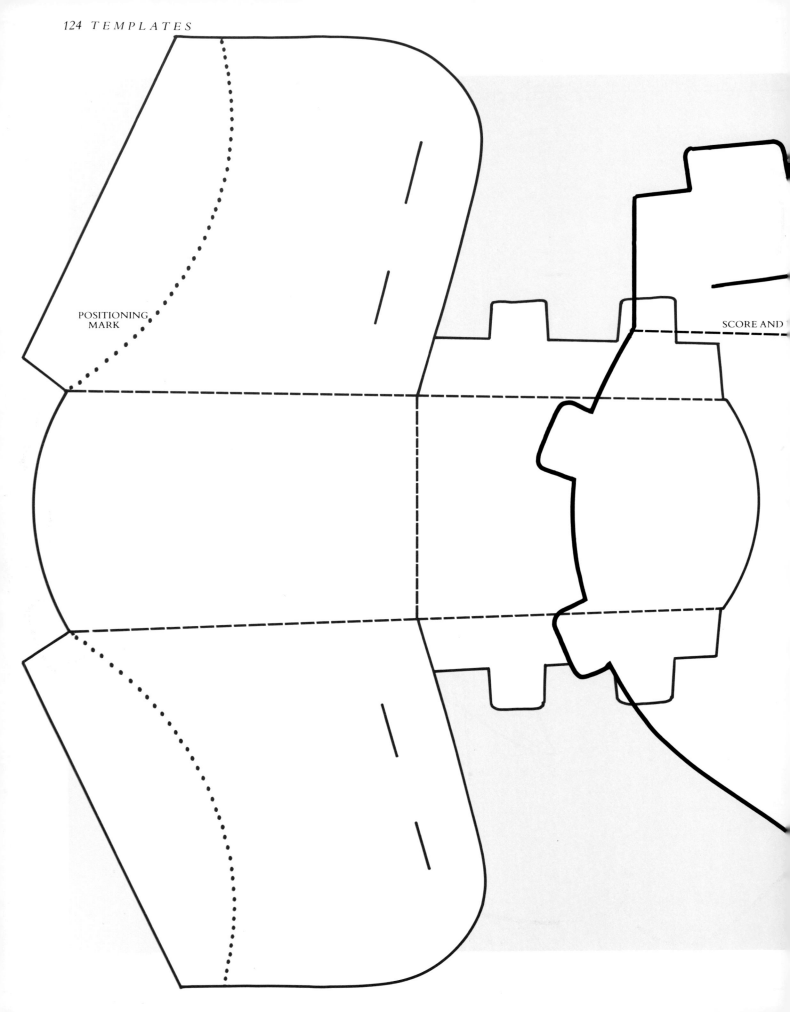

POSITIONING
MARK

SCORE AND

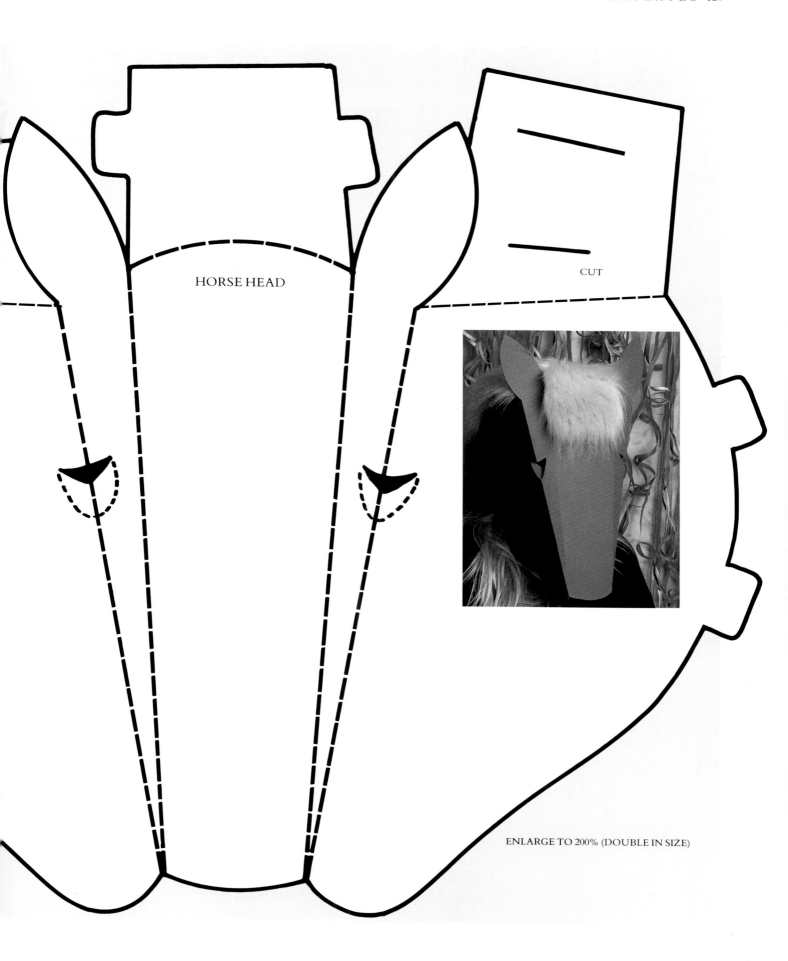

HORSE HEAD

CUT

ENLARGE TO 200% (DOUBLE IN SIZE)

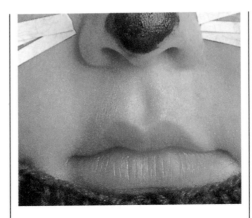

ACKNOWLEDGEMENTS

The authors and publishers would like to thank the following companies for their generosity in supplying materials used in the book:
Edding (UK) Ltd
Pick 'n' Choose
Threadbare
Oakley Fabrics Ltd
G. F. Smith & Son Ltd
Maple Textiles
Escapade
Philip & Tacey
For the loan of masks for photography many thanks to:
Zoe Addan
Linda Collins
Edward Levy
Gregory Warren Wilson
   The authors and publishers would also like to thank Julia Cousins, Pitt Rivers Museum; Christine DeCuir, Greater New Orleans Tourist and Convention Commission; Mary Dowling, Horniman Museum; Elizabeth Duff, Play Matters; Nancy Frazier, Museum Insights and Yvonne Schumann, Liverpool Museum; Florence Temko for invaluable assistance with research regarding North American museums, suppliers and background information; Diana Thomson for testing patterns; Marion Elliot for collaborating on the papier-mâché masks; Judith Simons; Marilyn Gasparini; Aurelio Campa and all those people who showed interest and gave us newspaper cuttings, catalogues and ideas. Finally, Peter, Caroline and Jacqueline Frank and George, Madeleine and Flora Kessler for their support and enthusiasm.
   The authors and publishers acknowledge the origami mask on page 79, designed by Florence Temko, author of many books on paper arts and folk crafts.

SUPPLIERS

United Kingdom
Most of the companies listed will be able to send you catalogues although sometimes there is a charge for this. There is usually a minimum quantity for mail order services but some of the companies welcome personal shoppers. Many of the materials used in this book will be available from your local department store, stationer or art and craft shop. For specialist supplies consult the Yellow Pages Directory. You could also look in needlecraft and hobby magazines.

Fantasy Fabrics,
Greenmantle, Plough Lane
Christleton, Chester CH3 7BA

Maple Textiles,
188-190, Maple Road
Penge, London SE20 8HT

Oakley Fabrics Ltd.,
8, May St
Luton, Bedfordshire LU1 3QY

Pick 'n' Choose,
The Craft People, 56 Station Rd
Northwich, Cheshire CW9 5RB

Threadbare,
Glenfield Pk, Glenfield Rd
Nelson, Lancashire BB12 9PG

Philip and Tacey,
North Way
Andover, Hampshire SP10 5BA

North America
For names of stores which handle mask supplies consult the Yellow Pages of the phone book under the following headings:
   Artists' Materials
   Costumes – Masquerades and Theatrical
   Craft Supplies

Leewards and Michael's are two large chains with many stores carrying a wide selection of handicraft materials. Call their corporate offices for the location of a store near you:

Leewards
100 St. Charles St
Elgin, IL 60120.
Phone 708/888-5800

Michael's
5931 Campus Circle Dr
Irving, TX 75063
Phone 214/580-6242

For mail order artists' and school supplies ask for a catalogue from:

Dick Blick
P.O. Box 1267
Galesburg, IL 61401
Phone 800/447-8192 (toll-free)

Daniel Smith
4130 First Ave So
Seattle, WA 98134
Phone 800/426-6740 (toll-free)

Also look in the small ads of craft magazines.

Models:
Maria Arbiter
Rebecca Dewing
Spencer Dewing
Caroline Frank
Madeleine Kessler
Janice Williamson

If this book has aroused your curiosity and you are interested in looking at historical and ethnic masks, ask at museums near you whether they have collections of masks and, if it is not on show, whether it would be possible to see them. Anthropological, folkcraft, ethnic and natural history museums would almost certainly have some masks and they would be able to tell you what is on show and to help you in other ways. Some museums have collections. Listed below you will find a limited selection of these museums.

UNITED KINGDOM

Liverpool Museum,
William Brown Street
Liverpool L3 8EN

The British Museum,
Great Russell St
London WC1

The Horniman Museum,
100, London Rd
London SE23 3PQ

The Museum of Mankind,
6, Burlington Gdns
London W1

Pitt Rivers Museum,
South Parks Road
Oxford OX1 3PP

NORTH AMERICA AND CANADA

Glenbow Museum
130 9th Avenue SE
Calgary, Alberta T2G 0P3

Field Museum of Natural History
Roosevelt Road at Lake Shore Drive
Chicago, IL 60605

Fowler Museum of Cultural History
University of California Los Angeles
Los Angeles, CA 90024

Louisiana State Museum
751 Charles St, PO Box 2458
New Orleans, LA 70176

Museum of American Folk Art
444 Park Ave South
New York, NY 10016

American Museum of Natural History
Central Park West at 79th St
New York, NY 10024

Metropolitan Museum of Art
5th Avenue at 82nd St
New York, NY 10028

Canadian Museum of Civilisation
100 Rue Laurier
PO Box 3100, Station B
Hull, Quebec J8X 4H2

Mummers Museum
Second St and Washington Ave
Philadelphia, PA 17147

North Carolina Museum of Art
2110, Blue Ridge Blvd
Raleigh, NC 27607

Asian Art Museum
Golden Gate Park
San Francisco, CA94118

Museum of International Folk Art
706 Camino Lejo, PO Box 2087
Santa Fe, NM 87504

Seattle Art Museum
Volunteer Park
Seattle, WA 98112

Royal Ontario Museum
100 Queen's Park
Toronto, Ontario M5S 2C6

UBC Museum of Anthropology
University of British Columbia
6393 Northwest Marine Drive
Vancouver, British Columbia
Z6T 1W5

Royal British Columbia Museum
675 Belleville St
Victoria, British Columbia V8Z 1X4

Smithsonian Institution
10th St and Constitution Ave NW
Washington, DC20560

BIBLIOGRAPHY

Alkema J. A., *Mask Making* (Sterling Publishing Co., NYC)

Bawden J., *The Art & Craft of Papier-Mâché* (Mitchell Beazley, London 1990)

Bihalji-Merin O., *Masks of the World* (Thames & Hudson, London 1971)

De La Porte Des Vaux D., *Masques aux Quatre Saisons* (Editions Fleurus, Paris)

Drew L., *Haida: Their Art and Culture* (Hancock House, 1982)

Duffek K., *Bill Reid: Beyond the Essential Form* (University of British Columbia Press, Vancouver 1986)

Ebin V., *The Body Decorated* (Thames & Hudson, London 1979)

Hardy A., *Mardi Gras Guide* (published annually by Arthur Hardy Enterprises Inc 4441 Iberville St, New Orleans, LA 70119 USA)

Jonaitis A., *From the Land of the Totem Poles* ([The N.W. Coast Indian Art Collection at the American Museum of Natural History] pub. American Museum of Natural History, NYC/ British Museum Publications, London 1988)

Kondeatis C., *Masks: Ten Amazing Masks to Assemble and Wear* (Pan, London and Sydney 1987)

Levi-Strauss C., *Structural Anthropology* (Penguin, London 1965)

O'Hanlon M., *Reading the Skin: Adornment, Display and Society among the Wangi* (British Museum Publications, London 1989)

Pegg B., *Rites and Riots: Folk Customs of Britain and Europe* (Blandford Press, Poole 1981)

Ray D. J., *Eskimo Masks* (Univ. of Washington Press, Seattle 1976)

Rinck M-P., *Macquillages Pour Jouer* (Editions Fleurus, Paris)

Segy L., *Masks of Black Africa* (Dover Publications, NYC 1976)

Snook B., *Making Masks* (Batsford, London 1972)

Statler O., *(Introduction) All Japan: The Catalogue of Everything Japanese* (Columbus, London/Quarto, NYC)

Stewart H., *Looking at Indian Art of the Northwest Coast* (Douglas and McIntyre, Vancouver and Toronto 1979)

Teuten T., *Masks: The Letts Guide to Collecting* (Letts, London 1990)

Wright L., *Masks* (Franklin Watts, London 1989)